THE LAST PURITAN?
ADLAI STEVENSON IN
AMERICAN POLITICS

RODNEY M. SIEVERS

National University Publications
ASSOCIATED FACULTY PRESS, INC.

Manufactured in the United States of America

Published by
Associated Faculty Press, Inc.
Port Washington, N.Y.

Library of Congress Cataloging in Publication Data

Sievers, Rodney M., 1943-
   The last Puritan?

   (National university publications)   Bibliography: p.
   1. Stevenson, Adlai E. (Adlai Ewing), 1900-1965.
2. Statesmen—United States—Biography.   3. United
States—Politics and government—1953-1961.
4. United States—Foreign relations—1961-1963.
5. United States—Foreign relations—1963-1969.
I. Title.
E748.S84S53   1983   973.921'092'4   83-2826

ISBN 0-8046-9318-8

FOR MY MOTHER AND
THE MEMORY OF MY FATHER

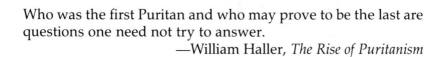

Who was the first Puritan and who may prove to be the last are questions one need not try to answer.

—William Haller, *The Rise of Puritanism*

ACKNOWLEDGMENTS

At various times, in different ways, the following persons encouraged me to write this book. I am deeply grateful to them all: Joseph R. Kett and William H. Harbaugh of the University of Virginia; Steve Fox, John Gimbel, Jack Hennessy, Roy Sundstrom, and Bill Tanner, friends and colleagues at Humboldt State University; William Dabney of the University of New Mexico; Ralph Dixon of Albuquerque, New Mexico, who first suggested I explore the subject of Adlai Stevenson; and Pete Brown, also of Albuquerque, a sustaining friend over the years.

Nancy Bressler and her staff at the Princeton University Library helped me to find my way through the imposing Stevenson papers. I am also grateful to the research staffs of the Illinois State Historical Library, the Wisconsin State Historical Library, and the Dwight David Eisenhower, Lyndon Baines Johnson, and Harry S. Truman Presidential Libraries. A grant from the National Endowment for the Humanities and a year's sabbatical leave from Humboldt State University provided time away from teaching duties to do research and write. Margie Rodgers typed the manuscript with professional skill and good cheer.

Finally, I wish to state my gratitude to those persons who kindly shared their recollections of Stevenson with me: the late Senator Clinton P. Anderson of New Mexico; the late Jacob M. Arvey; William McCormick Blair, Jr.; Jane Warner Dick; the Reverend Richard P. Graebel; Elizabeth Stevenson Ives; Margie Jones; Judge Carl McGowan; Arthur M. Schlesinger, Jr.; W. Willard Wirtz. Of course, all the opinions and judgments in these pages are my responsibility alone.

CONTENTS

INTRODUCTION

Long after midnight in the Chicago Amphitheater, on July 26, 1952, more than twelve hundred exhausted delegates to the Democratic National Convention, nearing the end of this quadrennial ritual, peered through the haze of the hot cavernous hall as their party's anointed standard-bearer delivered his acceptance address. Short, bald, somewhat diffident in manner, Adlai E. Stevenson at first glance was not a commanding presence. His party, moreover, was in serious trouble after twenty years of political ascendancy. Yalta, Alger Hiss, the "loss" of China, Korea—these ominous household words portended that, like the animals packed into the nearby Chicago stockyards, the assembled Democrats were facing a precarious future. But as Stevenson spoke, the weary delegates began paying closer attention to him. What they heard seemed more appropriate to a Puritan preacher than to a presidential candidate: "The ordeal of the twentieth century—the bloodiest, most turbulent era of the Christian age—is far from over. Sacrifice, patience, understanding and implacable purpose may be our lot for years to come. Let's face it. Let's talk sense to the American people. . . . Better we lose the election than mislead the people; and better we lose than misgovern the people." Adlai Stevenson lost the election but won the respect of millions of Americans. As the *New Republic* declared: "He set standards for moral courage that will inspire good men and haunt backsliders from this time forever forward."[1]

Almost exactly thirteen years later, on another scorching July day in Illinois, they brought him home to stay. President Johnson was one of the mourners; so was Secretary of State Rusk, who affirmed: "He not only spoke for his country, but . . . represented the essence of it. Our history, our traditions, our ideals, our aspirations were in his mind, his heart, and his very bones." Other tributes poured in from all over the world, honoring the memory of the man who had pledged to "talk sense."

Amid the chorus of eulogies, however, a few dissenting notes were struck. Murray Kempton, a long-time admirer, sadly observed that the "tragedy" of Stevenson's last years was that "for so many good reasons, he chose not to speak, and thus forfeited the right to be heard." "An attractive human being is gone. . . . But let us not delude ourselves as to what Adlai Stevenson signified," cautioned Irving Howe. "He was not a man of the left, not a traditional or even new-style American liberal. He was a man who tried to act by civilized standards in the present society, and he did not succeed." I. F. Stone delivered a harsher verdict: "The honors paid Stevenson by Johnson and Rusk attest the fact that he had allowed them to bury his integrity long before he died, a shadow of the man we once loved."[2]

While these comments were by no means typical, they foreshadowed the reaction against liberalism that would soon engulf segments of the intellectual community. Stevenson died in July 1965, a few months after the United States began the systematic bombing of North Vietnam, a few weeks before the outbreak of riots in the Watts section of Los Angeles, California. The fires in Southeast Asia and in the Black ghettoes consumed much of the credibility of liberalism and left it disoriented, vulnerable to attacks from both Left and Right. The radicalized journalist Jack Newfield, for example, recalled watching Stevenson at the United Nations in 1961 "lie his head off about America's role in the [Bay of Pigs] invasion. And so I began to learn what liberalism was all about." Even sympathetic writers have questioned Stevenson's lasting importance in American history. While acknowledging that his "very person seemed to exert a pull toward decency in public affairs," Joseph Epstein noted that there was little evidence that Stevenson had "a very precise idea of how American society was, or ought to be, organized." He was skeptical that Stevenson would be remembered as more than a "period politician." Arthur M. Schlesinger, Jr., who was one of Stevenson's staunchest supporters in the 1950s, has observed that "defeat, in a way, ended his life, and in his later years one often had the sense that he was only going through the motions." In 1976 Norman Cousins poignantly queried, "Does Anyone Remember A. E. S.?"[3]

During his lifetime Stevenson was generally scorned by conservatives, who seemed blind to his conservative instincts—which were many—and insisted on portraying him as a New Dealer—which he was not. Writing in the *National Review* in 1976, however, Adam Meyerson discovered praiseworthy elements in Stevenson's thinking: anti-Communism, commitment to fiscal restraint, emphasis on state and local government, and skepticism about expanding the sway of federal authority. Meyerson concluded that "whatever one may have thought of Stevenson at the time—and conservatives tended to think little of him—in retrospect he looks much better, and may even become a source of inspiration. . . ." When the political Right's view of Stevenson shows signs of softening, perhaps it is time to reexamine his significance.[4]

Thirty years have passed since he first ran for President. As Stevenson is increasingly perceived as a historical figure, new perspectives on his career will emerge. But the historian's responsibility remains constant: to explain men's ideas and actions in the context of their times. For Stevenson, that context was the political culture of the cold war, which enabled a man with fundamentally conservative instincts to be acclaimed as a hero by the liberal community. In the postwar era liberals attempted to adjust their political philosophy and strategy to fit the new realities of American life: cold war, McCarthyism, the rising prosperity of the middle class. Against this background of "affluence and anxiety," Stevenson twice ran for President, sought to hold his divided party together, and changed the tone of liberal politics in the United States.

I have not attempted to write a complete account of Stevenson's life and times. That task has been undertaken by John Bartlow Martin in his two-volume authorized biography, *Adlai Stevenson of Illinois* (1976) and *Adlai Stevenson and the World* (1977). Based on Stevenson's personal papers and extensive interviews with his friends and associates, it is a richly detailed work to which I am indebted in many ways. Thanks to Martin, we now know much more about Stevenson's private life. Martin also has excellent discussions of Stevenson's governorship, his two presidential campaigns, his "non-candidacy" in 1960, and his difficulties at the United Nations. Yet amid the wealth of information that the biography contains, interpretation is sacrificed to the sheer amount of factual data. One never learns exactly what Martin thinks of his subject; the reader finishes the book yearning for a conclusion that evaluates Stevenson's importance to American history.

My book is intended to meet that need. It is topically organized. The first chapter is a highly selective biographical essay, emphasizing those aspects of Stevenson's career that seem to me most relevant to the evolution of his public thought. The next three chapters focus on his principal concerns: the health of the American political system, the conduct of international relations, and the nature of the historical process. These matters were intricately interrelated in Stevenson's mind, reinforcing one another in subtle ways, but for purposes of analysis I have chosen to discuss them separately. In each chapter my main purpose is to show the relationship between what Stevenson believed and how he behaved, the linkage of thought and action. It is an important question in studying any public figure but especially so in Stevenson's case, because he was widely perceived as an "intellectual in politics." In fact, he was neither an original nor particularly profound thinker. But he was undeniably an intelligent, sensitive man, gravely worried about the major public issues of his day, even though his moral approach to politics caused him numerous difficulties and left some serious questions unanswered. I have tried to identify the essential elements in his thinking and to place his ideas and career in historical perspective. Many of the issues that concerned Stevenson, especially the awesome question of war and peace in the nuclear age, are no less pressing today than they were thirty years ago, when he emerged from relative obscurity and tried to "talk sense" to a troubled nation.

1

THE WELLSPRING OF A POLITICAL CAREER

ON HIS BIRTHDAY in 1947, a troubled Adlai Stevenson wrote in his diary: "Am 47 today—still restless; dissatisfied with myself. What's the matter? Wife, children, money, success—but not in law profession; too scattered in interests; how can I reconcile life in Chicago as lawyer with consuming interest in foreign affairs–public affairs and desire for recognition and position in that field?" When he learned that the United States Ambassador-designate to Great Britain had unexpectedly died, Stevenson's thoughts turned to the vacant position. "I *know* I could [do it] and its one of the few things I do *know* I could do," he reflected. "Maybe the time will come when Ellen would like to do something like that on a scale we could afford. But will I ever get the opportunities again—the way I have in the last year? Is it political stature I need or professional?"[1]

Two events in late 1948 and early 1949 irrevocably changed the course of Stevenson's life. The first was his election as governor of Illinois; the second was the collapse of his marriage of twenty years' duration. The governorship confirmed his love for public service and reinforced his long-standing political ambitions. The divorce freed him to pursue a political career, but at a stiff price; henceforth, even as "Adlai" became a household name, he felt lonely and isolated beneath his newly acquired renown. "I'm alone, utterly alone . . .

1

gloating in self-pity, oppressed with forebodings of disaster and dishonor," he confided to Jane Dick, one of his oldest friends and most loyal supporters, in March 1949. "Surrounded with everything for happiness and usefulness I'm desolate and destitute—and think of nothing except the creeping morrows. . . ." Ten years after the divorce, columnist Mary McGrory was impressed by its lasting impact on Stevenson. She said he told her that he accepted so many speaking engagements in part because "I have no life of my own."[2]

Stevenson frequently complained about the demands that politics made on him, but the reality was that he was irresistibly drawn to the political scene. The law was his vocation, but politics and public service were his calling. His perspective on events was shaped from deep within the partisan fray where, for all his protests, he felt most at home. Those who thought he was miscast in politics utterly misread the man, as his close friend Carl McGowan has repeatedly emphasized. Politics also enabled Stevenson to articulate the anxieties that increasingly permeated his thinking as time passed. Through the political process he acted out an inner necessity of his nature which he could express in no other way. For at heart he was a Puritan in politics, haunted by the dilemma of all Puritans over the ages—an acute awareness of the discrepancy between that which is and that which might be.

The years of World War II were challenging and exciting ones for Stevenson. From 1941 to 1946 he saw history being made, working for the federal government in various capacities: special assistant to the secretary of the navy, field agent for the Strategic Bombing Survey, special assistant to the secretary of state, participant in setting up the United Nations. Given his inherently restless nature, it is not surprising that following these heady experiences he had trouble readjusting to the lifestyle of a LaSalle Street lawyer. While many Americans gladly resumed their former careers after the war, Stevenson found "normalcy" tedious and unrewarding. Even before the war ended, he told the poet Archibald MacLeish (a friend and wartime colleague in the State Department) that he knew it was time to "get back to the prairies and act like a responsible husband, father, and breadwinner instead of a piece-work man in Washington," but then added, "I hope the Department will keep me in mind as an 'expert' on most anything. . . . it would make life on LaSalle street tolerable!"[3]

Stevenson was associated with one of the most prestigious law firms—Sidley & Austin—in Chicago; he was married to an attractive, intelligent woman, blessed with three healthy sons. A secure, prosperous future stretched out ahead of him in 1947 as the country turned its wartime arsenal to the production of peacetime goods for a generation of Americans who were about to enter "the best years of their lives," but Stevenson was a discontented man as his diary entries starkly reveal: "Too old and tired for these people—or something! Couldn't wait to leave" (after a boring social gathering). "Kellogg's for dinner—some old friends—pleasant, easy, relaxed feeling. Sad how little most of them have lived; done for their generation. Left early." And again: "Why don't I do what I want to do and like to do and is worthwhile doing?" What he wanted to do was to get into politics. By the end of 1947 he had done exactly that, but only through an unusual combination of circumstances.[4]

Stevenson had considered running for the United States Senate six years earlier, as he ruefully reported in 1942 to his friend Herman Dunlap ("Dutch") Smith. "The political pot has been boiling, and I have been conferring with a stream of Illinois statesmen. But the [Cook County Democratic] organization wouldn't have me—'not well enough known'—so they took . . . one of the boys." By 1947, however, "the boys" were in trouble, and suddenly they discovered new virtues in a candidate who was not identified with the organization.

The Cook County leader at the time was Colonel Jacob M. ("Jack") Arvey, to whom Stephen A. Mitchell, Louis Kohn, and Dutch Smith—Stevenson's principal boosters—made the case for their man throughout 1947. More than any other person, Jack Arvey made Stevenson's political career possible. He was interested in what Mitchell, Kohn, and Smith had to say about Stevenson because the Cook County machine had suffered major electoral setbacks in 1946. Then in 1947 Martin Kennelly, billed as a "reform" candidate, was elected mayor of Chicago. The lesson was not lost on Arvey as he looked ahead to the general election of 1948, which practically everyone expected to be a Republican year. Stevenson wanted to run for the Senate; he felt his government experience best qualified him for that position. But Arvey insisted that Paul H. Douglas, a University of Chicago economics professor with a distinguished combat record in the war, would stand a better chance against the incumbent, Senator C. Wayland Brooks, who liked to remind the voters of his exploits in World War I. Arvey and his Cook County associates may also have felt that they could not get along with Douglas as governor because he would oppose them on patronage. At any rate, Arvey decreed Stevenson must be the candidate for governor, because his "clean" image would be useful against Governor Dwight Green, the incumbent, whose administration had been marred by scandals.[5]

There is considerable irony in the fact that the man who would become a hero to liberals owed his start in politics to one of the urban political machines that Progressives had fought against since the turn of the century. Stevenson's presidential campaigns inspired the formation of political clubs in the suburbs and encouraged countless amateurs to go into politics, but he always maintained a good relationship with the old professional "pols" like Arvey, Richard Daley, and Pittsburgh's David Lawrence. He had no fundamental difference in principle with their brand of politics. Reviewing a book on the new politics by his former Democratic National Chairman, Steve Mitchell, in 1959, Stevenson remarked, "I hope the generation of the clubs proves as responsive to the political needs of the new times as the much maligned 'bosses' were to theirs."[6]

Despite the assurance of the organization's support, Stevenson equivocated right up to the last moment—a pattern that would characterize his behavior on other occasions in later years. He finally agreed to Arvey's stipulation in December 1947. "Well, I'm in it, after several days of indecision and stalling," he wrote on January 1 to his sister and brother-in-law. "I'm still a little stunned by the enormity of the task I've undertaken. Whether I've the strength, thick skin & capacity to at least make a good race I don't know, but at least I've got to try now for 10 fearful months. . . . I don't feel very gay this New Year's Day!"[7]

It was a curious way to launch a political career that he apparently had wanted for years, but personal problems also weighed heavily on Stevenson's mind at the outset of 1948. His marriage had never been an especially happy one. Probably the young couple had originally felt when they married in 1928 that they had much in common— Adlai an aspiring attorney, Ellen Borden the debutante daughter of a North Shore squire. But their relationship always seemed to lack something, some vital spark. "We *never* demonstrated affection in our family," Adlai III has recalled. "We were not a close family." Stevenson's wartime duties took him away from home for lengthy periods; Ellen, sharing none of her husband's enthusiasm for public service, began to cultivate her own artistic interests. Gradually they grew apart—a process that undoubtedly was accelerated by the war. Countless other couples had the same experience. For the Stevensons, as for many others, the result was divorce, although they stuck it out together until he was elected governor. Soon afterward Ellen left, taking their three children with her.[8]

Meanwhile, Stevenson had become romantically involved with another woman, Alicia Patterson, the tough-minded, strong-willed wife of millionaire Harry Guggenheim, with whom she founded the Long Island newspaper *Newsday*. She had known Stevenson years before in Chicago; they resumed their friendship when he was in New York, working at the United Nations, in the fall of 1947. The friendship quickly turned to love, in part because Alicia—unlike Ellen—reinforced Stevenson's political aspirations. "I wonder what the hell I'm doing and why—," he wrote her from the gubernatorial campaign trail in May 1948, "and then I think of you and that you think its good and worth while and wouldn't love me if I didn't behave this way—and then I get up and go at it again." "Was it all a dream?" he asked, following a rendezvous with Alicia in June. "Were you really here last week; did we really walk along the river bank together; did we really sit on the deck beneath the sky; did we cook supper together; did we conspire, plan, talk, worry, laugh—? Did we? did we? did we?" "Of course our lives are complicated. If they were not we wouldn't be we!" he reassured her in August. "Ah, what the hell am I saying. But you understand—we must look forward gaily, happily, hopefully—not backward, over just a few months— with 30 years to come." The day after his surprisingly decisive victory in November, he jubilantly reported to her, "I carried Ill. by 565,000 plus—never anything like it in history—515,000 ahead of Truman and 180,000 ahead of closest man on Democratic ticket. Now I'm really in trouble! But there are years and years and years ahead for us. I'll think no other way, if you don't mind."[9]

When Alicia abruptly informed Stevenson early in 1949 that she wished to end their relationship, her decision devastated him, particularly since it virtually coincided with Ellen's departure. (It is not clear whether Ellen knew of the affair.) In a pained, rambling reply to Alicia, he said that he had opened her letter "expecting that exultant feeling when its hard to swallow and keep composed—things like 'I've never loved anyone before' etc. . . .—Instead 'Okay, Lets be friends The whole business is kaput'. . . . Now I'm in my room—I've read it all and I'm a little sick. Moreover Adm. Jones of Great Lakes &

some Generals are downstairs waiting for dinner . . . and all the time about all I've known of love and genuine interest and personal concern for 10 years is—Kaput! . . . [but] I'm not resentful—I'm deeply grateful for even a few months of what was to be forever. And don't worry about me. Work has been my refuge for many years— now it will be for many more." The letter ended on a cryptic note. "So perhaps I've transgressed by not writing as I would rather do than anything else—as you well know—but there's only so much time, only so much strength—and now thats run out all over the floor— and I'm a mess and the butler's knocking—"[10]

Stevenson's prediction that work would be his refuge proved to be hauntingly accurate. Despite the fame he later acquired, and the abiding affection of family and close friends, he never filled the emotional vacuum that entered his life in 1949. In Springfield, he compensated by putting in long hours on state business. When his sister once urged him to get some rest after a hard day, he tersely replied, "I've failed as a husband. I've failed as a father. I will succeed as governor." "Never did I see a man in politics more conscientious," his friend Lloyd Lewis remarked in 1948. Stevenson's subsequent career suggests that in a sense he may have been too conscientious for his own good. "Life is 2/3 gone, & I don't know what I want or am trying to do," he reflected in 1950 to Alicia (who remained a favorite confidante until her death). Two years later he ran for President and found the recognition and fulfillment that he had sought for so long. But the price of fame was high. As Stevenson's reputation grew, so did a deep sense of responsibility which occasionally caused him to give the impression that all the world's problems rested on his shoulders. In a sympathetic sketch, the artist Ben Shahn depicted him as "a man of sorrows," troubled and mournful of countenance. "Sometimes I get a little frightened—," he once confessed to Agnes Meyer, "and when I do I feel very lonesome because no one else does or seems to and I suspect I must get things all out of proportion." "The one disappointment I have had in politics," he told an audience in 1957, ". . . is . . . in the feeling of frustration, of disillusionment, in not being able to get across in a political campaign ideas that have seemed to me part of the very warp and woof of civilization's survival." For this state of mind, Stevenson had only himself to blame. It was the consequence of his intensely moralistic view of politics, compounded by the persistent private loneliness that under-lay his public career.[11]

"For Stevenson there could be no 'moral holidays,' " Gordon Wilson Keller has noted, "no world worth having without risk." It was precisely the element of moral commitment in his thought that accounted for much of Stevenson's appeal to American liberals in the early 1950s, as they were reassessing the moral basis of their political philosophy in the aftermath of World War II. "I wonder if you know how many people pray for you," Stevenson asked the theologian Reinhold Niebuhr in 1952, saying that he felt "honored to be included as an irreverent member of that chorus." He had great respect for Niebuhr, whose blend of conservative theology and progressive politics set the tone for postwar liberalism. Writing in the *New Republic* in 1955, Niebuhr warned liberals not to permit what he termed the "errors of the Enlightenment" to "bedevil the 'progressive' political movement," or to allow themselves to be identified "with illusions about human nature and history." Yet Niebuhr was unwilling to abandon liberalism altogether, "because only that philosophy, stripped of its utopian errors, leaves the way to the future open."[12]

Similar sentiments pervaded the thinking of many liberals after the war: a conviction that in the past they had rested their political philosophy on a naïve view of human nature (savagely dispelled by Hitlerism and Stalinism); a determination to be henceforth more "realistic"; and a renewed faith in American democracy as the political system best equipped to lead the postwar world toward a better future. The cardinal virtue of the American political system, according to the liberal historian and political activist Arthur M. Schlesinger, Jr., in 1949, lay in its adherence to "the vital center"; i.e., preserving the delicate balance between the needs of society and the rights of the individual. Like Niebuhr, Schlesinger urged his fellow liberals to reject the myth of human perfection and get on with the hard job of defending freedom at home and abroad against totalitarianism of all varieties. Herein, he emphasized, was the realistic course of action for mid-century liberalism, having been "fundamentally reshaped by the hope of the New Deal, the exposure of [the true nature of] the Soviet Union, and by the deepening of our knowledge of man."[13]

Schlesinger's message was directed toward a generation of liberals whose faith in their cause had been severely tested by recent events. Liberals had rejoiced in the heady days of the early New Deal, when bold reform measures poured out of Washington and made Franklin D. Roosevelt's name synonymous with the progressive spirit. From the outset, however, the New Deal lacked a coherent philosophical underpinning; it was essentially a pragmatic program, heavily dependent on the President himself. Relatively little more was accomplished on the reform front after 1936, as an anti-New Deal conservative coalition formed in Congress and foreign affairs increasingly dominated Roosevelt's attention. When the New Dealers went marching off to war against Fascism, whatever reformist character the administration still possessed was lost. As Roosevelt said, "Dr. Win the War" had replaced "Dr. New Deal." FDR's death in 1945 quashed liberals' hopes that he might lead a resurgence of reform after the war. His successor in the White House valiantly sought to keep the reform impulse alive, but Harry Truman's Fair Deal did not fare well in Congress. Moreover, conservatives staged a strong political comeback in the 1946 midterm elections, and even after his stunning victory over Thomas E. Dewey in 1948, President Truman was regarded with suspicion, even hostility, by many liberals. Disoriented and dispirited, they clustered around "the vital center" and awaited a leader who could inspire them anew.

It was to this generation of liberals that Stevenson appealed so powerfully when he ran for President in 1952. His mild progressivism and conservative instincts reflected their own state of mind. One admiring writer, pointing out that Stevenson had a "deep awareness of man's painfully divided nature, where the Enlightenment saw only good," described him as "an eloquent spokesman for that 'vital center' where moderates from both left and right can meet." Perhaps only in the distended political atmosphere of the early 1950s, when the very word "liberal" was suspect in some quarters and the forces of reaction were on the rise, could liberals have hailed so conservative a person as their champion. He was remote—by experience, temperament, and interest—from the bread-and-butter issues that had characterized Democratic party politics for the preceding half century. Unlike Truman, he had never known economic hardship at first hand. Unlike Roosevelt, he had no imaginative empathy with the concerns of the workers and the dispossessed. He had little if any sense of where he thought the party should be headed at this critical juncture in its history. Yet, as one of his friends warned him early in 1952, he was "tapped" to "preserve liberalism and carry it forward. . . ." It was a dubious charge for a LaSalle Street lawyer.[14]

He was first "tapped" by none other than the President himself. In January 1952 Truman apparently told Stevenson that he could be nominated by the Democrats with Truman's full support. Stevenson, according to Truman, was "flabbergasted" by the suggestion and put the President off. The next morning Stevenson called another of his wartime friends, George W. Ball, and told him that he had " 'made a hash' of his talk with the President, who had not understood his feelings at all. . . ." Truman certainly did not understand Stevenson; they were totally different types of persons. Eric Sevareid pinpointed the gulf between them when he observed that to Truman "liberalism means a set of concrete projects; to Adlai Stevenson it means a state of mind, a morality of tolerance and humanity. . . ."[15]

Many factors contributed to Stevenson's reluctance to run for President in 1952, the principal reason being the one that he repeatedly stated between January and July: his desire to seek reelection as governor of Illinois. Of course, he was aware that the upcoming election did not look promising for the Democrats, with Truman's popularity at an all-time low and the Korean War dragging on with no end in sight. He felt that, should he become the party's choice, his best chance to win in the fall depended on not being perceived as "Truman's candidate." Also, according to Carl McGowan, Stevenson initially felt it might be good if the Republicans recaptured the White House after twenty years, because he feared that they were growing increasingly irresponsible in their criticism. (That view, however, was predicated on the premise that the GOP would not nominate an "Old Guard" spokesman like Senator Robert A. Taft of Ohio, whom Stevenson saw as an irreconcilable reactionary.) "I just don't want to go for it; I wouldn't be honest with myself if I did and I attach importance to the inconsistency of being a candidate for Gov. of Ill. and publicly or even privately running for Pres.," he explained to Alicia Patterson in March 1952. "I just can't seem to get over that hurdle which no one seems to understand—even if I wanted to run for Pres. which I don't."[16]

On March 29, President Truman—(who had been defeated in the New Hampshire primary by Senator Estes Kefauver of Tennessee)— announced that he would not seek another term. A few days later, Stevenson was renominated for governor. On April 16, he issued a statement declaring that he "could not accept the nomination for any other office this summer." "This is the hardest thing I have ever had to do," he wrote Truman, "but, as I told you at Blair House, I could see no best way out of my dilemma, and this seemed to me the right way in all the circumstances." Three months later he was nominated for President.[17]

There is no need to explain what happened in terms of some subtle or devious strategy on Stevenson's part. He did not want to run in 1952. He was nominated because (1) no one else emerged as a viable candidate in the period between April and July, (2) an independent "Draft Stevenson" committee, formed in February, worked on his behalf all summer, seeking to publicize his name and familiarize the delegates to the national convention with his record, (3) Truman and the party powers that be did not oppose his nomination when as the Alsop brothers wrote, "it became clear that the convention wanted Stevenson and nobody else"; (4) Stevenson never said he would refuse a draft, thinking it was unlikely to happen. "I want so much to stay here [Springfield] and do this job that I asked for better than its ever been done before," he told Alicia in late June. ". . .but at the same time if the country really needs me, if theres [sic] a touch of destiny about the draft business, than I don't want to thwart it and make a tragic mistake." Forces were closing in on him, pointing irresistibly to the outcome at the convention in Chicago, where he was nominated on the third ballot. "If there ever was a genuine draft for the office of President," Jack Arvey insisted almost twenty years later, "Governor Stevenson was the subject of it." On July 26 he accordingly accepted his party's most coveted prize without having even campaigned for it. If Stevenson convinced himself that there was "a touch of destiny" surrounding his career, who could refute the idea?[18]

The delighted liberals certainly were not so inclined. Inspired by Stevenson's stirring acceptance address to the convention, they rushed to bestow the Roosevelt mantle on this newcomer from the Lincoln country, whether it fitted him or not. "Stevenson's voice at its finest is like the violin note that frees itself from the other music and goes on alone," rhapsodized TRB in the *New Republic*. Asserting that the American people would "never tire of reform, progress and social betterment," he proclaimed that Stevenson was "more like a Roosevelt 'braintruster' than the amiable, non-cerebrating type of palace crony with which we have become familiar [in the Truman administration]." But Stevenson did not regard himself as a New Dealer. In fact, he did not seem to know *what* he was in terms of political philosophy. When Samuel Rosenman, FDR's old adviser, asked Stevenson to clarify his attitude toward the New Deal, he cautiously replied that he felt "no reluctance about identifying myself with the Roosevelt regime . . . [but] I must keep in character, and I am a moderate, I suppose." If anything, he seemed to identify most closely with Woodrow Wilson's New Freedom philosophy of 1912–1916, which emphasized restoring economic competition and using the federal government as a policeman in society, to be invoked when needed and then—ideally—withdrawn. Stevenson's experience as governor had given him a state-oriented viewpoint which set him apart from the New Dealers. In speeches during the late forties and early fifties he hammered away at the need to restore vitality to the local and state governments, not in the name of states' rights (which had a regional, negative connotation) but in that of what he termed "states' responsibilities."[19]

Such thinking hardly placed Stevenson in the New Deal–Fair Deal tradition. James Reston accurately observed that both candidates in 1952 were political "middle-of-the-roaders, [Dwight] Eisenhower to the left of his party, and Stevenson to the right of the New Deal, further to the right than most people realize." One must remember that the country was undergoing a conservative reaction, haunted by cold-war inspired fears of the Russians abroad and the specter of McCarthyism at home. Under such circumstances, Stevenson could not have afforded to campaign as a New Dealer–Fair Dealer even had he so desired. Besides, as Alonzo Hamby has emphasized, the vital center as outlined by Niebuhr and Schlesinger "was not a new liberal *program*" but rather "a new *mood*." Here again, Stevenson was in tune with the times because he thought of liberalism—insofar as he thought of it at all—less as an economic doctrine than as a pluralistic philosophy aimed at maximizing individual freedom, almost in the classical nineteenth-century sense. As he told the New York Liberal party, "It seems to me that an authentic humility, an awareness of the complexity of men's choices, a tolerance for diverse opinions, and a recognition for brave experimentation are the heart of any liberal faith." That was exactly what the vital center was all about.[20]

Throughout the campaign Stevenson labored under the handicap of having to defend the record of the Truman administration, including the Korean conflict. He also was up against an inordinately popular opponent in the person of Eisenhower. "I Like Ike" was a potent psychological solution to the "K_1C_2" (Korea, Communism, corruption) formula devised by the Republicans against the Democrats, even if the general had no clear idea what he would do about Korea, Communism, or corruption. Eisenhower probably assured victory for himself by announcing shortly before the election that he would "go to Korea" if elected, implying that he would find a way to end the war. Still, Stevenson remained optimistic about his chances, perhaps remembering his stunning upset victory in Illinois four years earlier; on election night he privately predicted that he would win with a total of 325 electoral votes. He did receive a popular vote of over twenty-seven million, but he got only eighty-nine electoral votes and carried just nine states, all in the Solid South. It was a personal triumph for Eisenhower, but it was also something more than that. While the Democrats were reluctant to acknowledge the fact, "modern Republicanism," by its de facto acceptance of an enlarged role for the federal government in social and economic matters, had preempted much of liberalism's territory. The Democrats, by contrast, had nothing new to offer the electorate. Stevenson injected a fresh personality into the campaign and delivered some eloquent speeches, but his political program amounted to little more than a warmed-over version of Wilsonian progressivism without its sense of urgency concerning economic inequities. He thus failed to furnish his party with a new sense of direction or purpose at a time when the opposition seemed to have rejuvenated itself behind Ike and "modern Republicanism."[21]

Stevenson's defeat did not diminish the liberals' expectations for him. Arthur Schlesinger, Jr., who worked in the campaign, knew that liberalism needed a major overhaul after the 1952 election, and he still looked to Stevenson to lead the way. "Because Stevenson understands the hard job of rethinking and reformulation which lies ahead, he represents perhaps the most creative force in American politics today; he is the voice of the post-Roosevelt epoch," wrote Schlesinger. "For it is only as it expresses the possibilities of the future—and not as it revives the memories of the past—that progressivism can once again recover its central place in American life." Other voices soon joined the chorus. Journalist Richard H. Rovere asserted that Stevenson "looks forward eagerly to the job of helping American liberalism to restate its ends and to seek new, appropriate means." In a letter to Stevenson, Eric Sevareid declared: "You can reorganize and revitalize the Democratic party in the name of the young and the hopeful. . . . There is no other effective national champion of civil liberties, of free speech, of the true American liberal movement except yourself." The former New Deal administrator David E. Lilienthal told him, "It is my hope that you will carry on, speaking for all the rest of us who believe in the America you believe in, who are moved by the eloquence and insight with which you express our own aspirations. . . ." The liberal columnist Gerald W. Johnson expressed his view of the situation more bluntly: "American liberalism is a chicken with its head cut off. Your function is to stick its head back on."[22]

It was one thing for Stevenson to ride to the liberals' rescue in their hour of need in 1952. It was quite another matter for them to expect him to redefine their political creed. Programmatic or creative thinking was not Stevenson's forte, and in this respect he was unsuited to the herculean task they demanded of him. "I think you both misjudge my talents and my temperament," he cautioned one enthusiastic correspondent. ". . . I am not a fearless, tireless knight and find the bright lights distasteful and the trumpets a little chilling. Perhaps one gets this way after some 12 years of almost ceaseless and sleepless public work." "The problem of 'party leadership' has infinite difficulties and hazards, . . ." he commented to Eric Sevareid, "particularly if one has no further political ambitions and a great desire to come to rest in some work both useful, permanent, stable and profitable!"[23]

Having once entered the political limelight, however, Stevenson quickly discovered he could not simply retire to the sidelines, even had he been so inclined. He was less than candid when he told Sevareid that he had "no further political ambitions." Politics was in his blood. A six-month global tour to Asia, the Middle East, and Europe in 1953 kept his name in the news, while impressing on him at first hand the profound problems and importance of the so-called underdeveloped countries. Henceforth this became one of his standard themes. *Look* magazine gave him further publicity by publishing a series of articles concerning his impressions of the places he visited. Back home, he found the practice of the law no more rewarding than before, while the return of the Republicans to power offered him an inviting target for verbal sharpshooting. Soon Stevenson was on the road again, delivering sharp partisan attacks on the new administration. Perhaps the most important of these speeches occurred at a party fund-raising dinner in Miami early in 1954 when he accused the administration of employing McCarthy-like tactics to weed out alleged "security risks" from government jobs. "A political party divided against itself, half McCarthy and half Eisenhower, cannot produce national unity—cannot govern with confidence and purpose," he declared. Charging that the loyalty clearance program was politically motivated to appease the Republican right wing, he affirmed that the "end result . . . is a malign and fatal totalitarianism." He ignored the fact that loyalty checks on federal employees had begun under President Truman. The Miami speech drew considerable attention, much of it positive, from the national press. It served notice that Stevenson had no intention of fading away. As he assumed the role of foremost critic of the administration he became the early front-runner for the Democratic nomination in 1956.[24]

Actually he was not enthusiastic about the prospect of running against Eisenhower again, but the logic of events increasingly pointed in that direction. In a letter written early in 1954 to Carl McGowan, urging the Stevenson camp to cultivate the support of the Speaker of the House, Sam Rayburn, the veteran Democratic professional James Rowe, Jr., said he realized that Stevenson might be "disinterested" in such matters at the moment, but predicted that "fate and circumstance will make him [interested] eventually. . . ." During the next two years "fate and circumstance"—augmented by his reluctance to retire to private life—propelled Stevenson toward a rematch with Eisenhower in 1956. The most significant of those fateful circumstances were (1) the U.S. Supreme Court's school desegregation ruling in 1954, which magnified the deep division within the Democratic party between its northern and southern wings and underscored the need to nominate someone acceptable to both camps in 1956; (2) Stevenson's vigorous role in the 1954 midterm elections; he campaigned widely for Democratic candidates and was credited with helping the party regain control of Congress; (3) President Eisenhower's heart attack in 1955, which initially appeared to rule him out of the 1956 race; (4) the insistence of various party leaders that Stevenson had an obligation to run again; as Jack Arvey later explained, had Stevenson "bypassed the 1956 campaign and run in 1960 he . . . would have been termed an ingrate by the rank and file of the Democratic Party"; (5) his personal loneliness and restlessness, which continued to feed Stevenson's political ambitions; (6) his intense partisanship, which bred a growing conviction that the Eisenhower administration was a disaster for the country. "There is no novelty or honor in a repeat performance," he told Gerald Johnson in 1955. "Of one thing I am positively sure, I want to beat the Republicans more than to advance Stevenson." But it was not hard to persuade himself that the two objectives might go hand in hand.[25]

At a strategy meeting at his home in August 1955, Stevenson sought out the opinions of various advisers concerning the political situation in 1956. One of those present was Newton N. Minow, who had worked in the 1952 campaign and subsequently become a law partner of Stevenson's. "I was against his running for President for the same reason that I had been in '52—I thought it was a lost cause," Minow recalls. "But the rest all thought he was the party's best; Eisenhower was a disaster; the prospect of [Richard] Nixon was even worse. He had to run. It was pretty well decided that he was going to do it. But he kept saying, 'Not unless the party wants me.' " It soon became evident that most of the party hierarchy did want him, and Stevenson received the impression he could be nominated without much opposition. But then, on September 24, 1955, President Eisenhower suffered a heart attack while vacationing in Colorado, and overnight the political scene dramatically shifted. Now, much to Stevenson's chagrin, other Democratic hopefuls began to make their availability known, since the nomination obviously would be a far more desirable prize if Eisenhower were unable to run. Returning from a political mission to Texas, where he gave a speech and visited the Senate majority leader, Lyndon Johnson—who was also recuperating from a heart attack—Stevenson bitterly complained to Newton Minow, "They told me that I must run in the primaries. They told me that with Eisenhower sick there's going to be a lot of candidates and if I want the nomination I have to go into the primaries." When Minow concurred with this assessment of the situation, Stevenson retorted, "Then I'm not running. I have no interest in this. I'm not running for sheriff. If the party wants me I'll go run—but I'm not going to those supermarkets."[26]

Stevenson had been spoiled by the unique circumstances surrounding his baptism into presidential politics in 1952, when the desperate Democrats practically forced the nomination upon him. Now he reacted like a pampered child when he realized that he would have to fight for it. "I'm a little irked by the goings on in N.Y.," he wrote to Alicia Patterson in October concerning Averell Harriman's presidential maneuverings. ". . . it will not be easy for a Democrat, any Democrat, to win, with or without Ike," he emphasized. "And now, to exploit an outside chance, A. H. is kicking away the first chance in modern times for a major party out of office to agree on its candidate 10 months in advance. . . ." As he told Minow, Stevenson dreaded the prospect of battling his way through the primaries. But ambition and a sense of obligation prevailed. Instead of declining to run, as he had threatened, he formally announced his candidacy on November 15, 1955. "I have 'gone and done it,' " he afterward explained to a friend, "not with any weary sense merely of doing my duty nor with any great exhilaration, but with a comfortable feeling that it is right and that it has fallen to my lot in my generation to do all I can to preserve the dialogue that makes democracy work. . . ." But he cited less lofty reasons in a letter to Archibald MacLeish in the midst of the primary election gauntlet a few months later. "You are right . . . about the sense of obligation. There was no other reason [to run] this time, and the obligation was mighty articulate from many quarters." Still, he did not have to do it. More ambitious than he ever cared to admit, Stevenson invariably cited "pressures" to explain his decisions at critical moments in his political career—in 1947, 1952, 1955, and 1960. But the truth is that he invited most of those pressures by making it known that he was "available." In fact, the real pressure, as with most politicians, was self-generated.[27]

It is also true that many people in the Democratic party strongly urged him to run in 1956, as he claimed. A broad spectrum of moderate and liberal Democrats saw him as the party's only hope for the fall. To a moderate Southerner like Harry S. Ashmore of the *Arkansas Gazette*, Stevenson was the one candidate whose nomination would not destroy the party. "If . . . the Northern partisans carry a deadlocked convention for one of their own, the odds are long that a massive Southern bolt will develop, possibly spelling the permanent division of the party," Ashmore warned him. ". . . you must emerge as the only Democrat in sight who can unite the Party and hold it together in the election ahead." Meanwhile, Northern liberals renewed their call for Stevenson to use the campaign to articulate "a new definition of American political liberalism, adequate to today's challenge," as Connecticut's Chester Bowles put it. But how could any meaningful reaffirmation of liberalism fail to take into account the ominous issue of civil rights for Black Americans? And how could the Democratic candidate do that without further dividing—even destroying—the party? Whereas Stevenson had been to a large extent his own man in the 1952 campaign, the politics of 1956 forced him into the more conventional role of trying to be all things to all men— or at least to all Democrats.[28]

Civil rights was becoming a momentous issue in the country by 1956, but Stevenson—like many politicians in both parties—did not appreciate its urgency. Politically related caution, a gradualist view of social change, and paternalistic attitude toward Blacks conditioned his thinking. He actually believed that civil rights activists were trying to change race relations too quickly. In this respect Stevenson's views disturbed Democrats like Harry Truman, Hubert Humphrey, and Herbert Lehman, who were more sensitive to Blacks' grievances. In 1955 a young Black named Emmet Till was kidnapped and murdered in Mississippi; his probable killers were subsequently acquitted. When liberals like James Wechsler and Arthur Schlesinger, Jr., asked Stevenson to speak out more forcefully on the case, he replied to Schlesinger that "I hardly know what Mr. Wechsler would want me to do, unless it was just shout, which helps things very little even if it pleases some Negro leaders. . . ." For someone who regularly stressed the moral aspect of political issues, Stevenson had a curious lack of moral passion about civil rights.[29]

He finally clinched the nomination after turning back Estes Kefauver's vigorous challenge in the primaries, but Stevenson emerged from what he called "this insane endurance contest" depleted in both physical strength and fresh ideas before the autumn contest against Eisenhower—who had made a rapid recovery, much to the Republicans' relief—even got under way. "If it hadn't been for that six months primary ordeal, I wouldn't feel so squeezed and wasted," he told Archibald MacLeish. And he admitted to Agnes Meyer that "I'm tired and don't feel the old urge to say everything just right as I used to."[30]

As early as 1954 Stevenson had asked Thomas K. Finletter, who headed up an informal group of liberal brain trusters for the Democrats, to organize a policy planning staff to assist the party's candidate in 1956. "My point is that there is a vast amount of imaginative work to be done," he reminded Finletter, "if we are going to have anything resembling a coherent, well-thought out party 'program' . . . a year and a half hence." Although the Finletter group did supply him with position papers on various issues in subsequent months, Stevenson's desire for a "coherent party program" remained unfulfilled on the eve of the campaign. (Perhaps he should not have been so surprised. Who has ever associated coherence with the Democratic party?)[31]

The Democratic campaign theme in 1956 was a variety of reform proposals based on the idea that dire economic distress had been largely eliminated. The so-called New America program called for improving the "quality" of life and targeted several areas for improvement: education, medical care, the plight of the elderly, conservation of natural resources, urban redevelopment. But the divisive civil rights issue was not given a prominent place on the Democratic agenda, and foreign affairs was downplayed because Stevenson's advisers insisted that President Eisenhower was invincible in that area.

It is difficult to say exactly how much Stevenson himself contributed to the New America program. Its assumption of an expanded role for the federal government in social policy ran counter to Stevenson's former emphasis on the responsibilities of state government. The architects of the New America program were liberal brain trusters, like Arthur Schlesinger, Jr., John Kenneth Galbraith, Seymour Harris, Robert Tufts, and others, who felt that Americans now suffered more from psychological malaise than from hunger and cold. Schlesinger, in particular, argued that the traditional rhetoric of reform was unsuited to the times. In a lengthy memorandum he prepared for Stevenson in 1955, analyzing the 1956 political situation, Schlesinger cautioned that Truman-style talk, giving the Republicans hell over bread-and-butter issues, "only sounds like Populist demagogy today." If the New America program was intended to provide a more sophisticated approach to reform, however, it turned out to be too sophisticated for the Democrats' own good. Stevenson's failure at the polls in 1956 made a mockery of Schlesinger's confident assertion: "A leader who could convince the nation that 'our future is what we make it' ought to find a ready response. . . ."[32]

Initially Stevenson shared the liberals' expectations for the campaign. "I want to develop the new America theme," he explained to Gerald Johnson soon after the Democratic convention, "because it seems to me the root of the trouble is a total failure of vision, total dedication to the advertising arts, total indifference to man's deeper sympathies and wants, and, finally, a failure to exploit the great opportunities of this fork of history." But he failed to communicate these sentiments during the months that followed. Perhaps such ideas do not lend themselves to political discourse. Perhaps he was just too tired after the primaries. Perhaps he had lost confidence in what he was saying. At any rate, the fundamental premise of the campaign—that liberalism must move beyond the New Deal and address itself to the "qualitative" problems of society—fell for the most part on inattentive ears.

Stevenson's speeches, moreover, seemed to lack the zest that had characterized his public addresses four years earlier. To the *Nation* it amounted to a disappointing performance. "Compared to 1952, this was a campaign without imagination, without conviction, without spirit, and most of all, without idealism," the magazine lamented. It was also one of the most mismanaged campaigns in American history, with liberal intellectuals and professional politicians contending with one another for the candidate's ear, while President Eisenhower sat serenely above the turmoil behind the reassuring slogan of "peace and prosperity." Stevenson did inject controversy into the campaign when he suggested that the military draft be terminated and that the United States consider halting atmospheric nuclear-weapon tests. But both proposals backfired on him. The eruption of international crises in the Middle East and Hungary shortly before the election merely added to Eisenhower's electoral margin. Stevenson never had a chance.[33]

Afterward, Schlesinger and Seymour Harris defended the New America concept in the introduction to a collection of Stevenson's campaign speeches. Their comments reveal the dilemma of the liberals during the Eisenhower years.

> It is often said that liberalism needs new ideas and new programs—that it has subsisted too long on memories of the New and Fair Deals. While no doubt there is something in this, we are not sure that this is liberalism's central problem. What liberalism perhaps needs even more is a new and compelling vision of the decent society to enable us to revalue our lives and redirect our energies. . . . Spiritual unemployment can be as real and as painful a fact as economic unemployment. By any reasonably sensitive barometer, the times are out of joint. The moment is surely approaching for a new forward surge of liberalism. It will probably not come, as did the New Deal, from the breakdown of the economic system. It will more likely come, as did the Progressive movement of the turn of the century, from an attempt to meet the moral needs of a people beset by psychological unrest and anxiety.[34]

This curious *apologia* probably offered little comfort to Stevenson in the wake of his shattering defeat. The truth of the matter was that such issues as "spiritual unemployment" left most voters cold. As one critic has observed, the liberal intellectuals had unwittingly "confounded their own position with that of the country, and equated their own dissatisfaction with the needs of the population."

What the liberal intellectuals sought from Stevenson "first and fore-most was public token of their superiority to their less-educated countrymen," another critic, Midge Decter, charged. When Steven-son failed to validate that superiority at the polls, "the failure was taken to be his in the doing, not theirs in the being. As early as 1953, one began to hear it said of him that he was a 'loser.' . . ."[35]

Only during the Progressive era before World War I, as Schlesinger and Harris acknowledged, have Americans supported reform politics in a time of economic growth. In 1956 the American electorate demonstrated that it was satisfied with the quality of American life by reelecting Eisenhower in a landslide. (Eisenhower: 35,590,472; 457 electoral votes; Stevenson: 26,029,752; 73 electoral votes. Eisenhower even dented the Solid South, carrying six southern states.) As *Newsweek* magazine declared: "Never since '32 have Americans felt more secure—both as a nation and as individuals; never since then has 'the American way of life' seemed more permanent—or more desirable." But the liberals—and Stevenson—refused to recognize the legitimacy of this perspective on the national condition; they insisted it was all an illusion, a facade, a sleight of hand trick perpetrated by the Republicans' public-relations managers. Insofar as Stevenson shared this belief, he misread the feelings of the average American as much as his liberal brain trusters did, and he thus must share some of the responsibility for the Democratic disaster.[36]

Afterward he was more upset than he admitted. Twice he had been rejected by the American people for the highest elective office. "The Gov. took this one hard," Newton Minow remarked. "He knew he was through in terms of ever being President." Stevenson soon announced that he would not seek the Presidency again. As for the 1956 debacle, "it *was* duty—the urgings of the [party] leaders thru 1955—that made me do it," he insisted to Agnes Meyer. His future plans were once more up in the air, but again numerous persons implored him to remain active in public affairs. "You say you are not going to run again. Fine. What this country needs desperately is a self-starting . . . hell-raiser who is not running for anything," Gerald Johnson told him. "You have no need to cultivate either Southern Bourbons or Northern bosses, yet you have the ear of the country." But could a twice-defeated candidate keep the ear of the country—even assuming he had it—for long? "How and whether to try to exercise any moral influence in the party ideologically or in the succession is a question that perplexes me," Stevenson told James

Wechsler of the *New York Post*, "but for the moment I am going to 'forsake the hot debate and walk beneath the stars and listen.' "[37]

But not indefinitely. Quiet contemplation was not in his nature. Besides there was his much-abused law practice to attend to. During the next three years he concentrated on private business and made fewer overtly political speeches. He served on the boards of the Field Foundation and the *Encyclopaedia Britannica*. He continued to travel widely—Europe, Africa, Russia, the Caribbean, plus innumerable trips around the country, combining business, politics, and pleasure. As Newton Minow succinctly put it, "Those were the good days . . . the prosperous years." Stevenson seemed genuinely relieved to be free of the unremitting political demands he had lived under since 1948. "I am not trembling with apprehension that that sheriff's posse bristling with shotguns is likely to come and get me," he wrote to Gerald Johnson in 1957. "For me it will be the law business, with an occasional [political] utterance, and some concentration on foreign affairs, which was my first interest." He liked to think of himself as a spokesman for the public interest, a sort of modern-day common-wealth man. When Oxford University bestowed an honorary degree on him in 1957, he seized the opportunity to deliver a lengthy address on international affairs, emphasizing the growing importance of the former colonial areas of the world. He enjoyed these kinds of speeches. They reinforced his view of himself as a statesman and critic-at-large.[38]

Although the late fifties were unquestionably good years for him in some respects, Stevenson was still a lonely man. During these years, he carried on an extensive correspondence with Agnes Meyer, the wife of the publisher of the *Washington Post* and a self-styled political guru in Democratic circles. Mrs. Meyer appears to have served as a surrogate mother figure for Stevenson. He shared some of his inner-most thoughts with her, and she sent him long handwritten letters alternately encouraging and reprimanding him. "Yes . . . I think that God *did* send you to me," he wrote her early in 1957. ". . . surely the sense of purpose, of mission and the confidence & strength you've given me in these trying years . . . was a fortification, a reinforce-ment, that I sorely needed. . . ." When she once told him that in her opinion he was not a very good prospect for any woman to marry, he asked in reply, "Isn't there something to be said for the proposition that *until* I'm married . . . I won't get what you call my 'ego-ambitions' (I say, *if any!*) into balance . . .?" He added that it was "not easy to wholly dismiss the idea of marriage as you enjoin me because I would make a bad husband when my best chance of being a proper person and fulfillment *is* by love and marriage." But he ruefully admitted, "It would have to be the right kind of person, and there's none in sight! So I'll have to slow my pace . . . and that, my dear friend, is not easy for me. . . . The pressures from all sides go on and on." Yet Stevenson thrived on those pressures, as Mrs. Meyer reminded him. "You cannot afford to be inactive, as a more philosophical temperament might," she pointed out. "You will churn around between alternatives, become restless, dissatisfied and aware of your ever-threatening solitude. . . ." Her analysis was correct. An awareness of "ever-threatening solitude" had underscored Stevenson's political career from the outset. It continued to do so right to the end.[39]

A continuing source of unhappiness for him was the erratic behavior of his former wife. Ellen was betraying symptoms of the mental illness that eventually led to her being placed in an institution. She was prone to making irrational accusations against other members of the family and caused some embarrassing scenes. When the Stevensons' son John Fell was married in 1962, Ellen attended the ceremony; Stevenson noted cryptically afterward, "Ellen I'm sure I never met before." Yet, when traveling abroad he sometimes referred to earlier visits to the same places "with Ellen." He was haunted by the past.[40]

As the Eisenhower era drew to a close, Stevenson kept a close eye on the battle shaping up within the Democratic ranks for the 1960 presidential nomination, even though he had forsworn making another bid for the White House. "The horizon for next year approaches faster than I like to contemplate and seems to include more and more politics," he informed Ellen's aunt Lady Mary Spears, in late 1959. "Three years ago . . . it seemed impossible that I might even be discussed [for President] let alone involved again. I am going to do my best to discourage both!" The bite of the presidential bug, however, leaves its victims with a recurring fever. Although Stevenson repeatedly insisted that he wanted no part of it all, the fact was that it had all become too much a part of him. When he told Agnes Meyer in 1959 to stop running him for President, she astutely replied that "you are running as hard as you can, both consciously and unconsciously." He was indeed irresistibly drawn to the political wars, and as always, he was encouraged by others to get involved. One of them was Mrs. Meyer, who while berating Stevenson for his indecision, kept urging him to pursue the nomination. Early in 1960, for example, she told him in no uncertain terms, "Adlai, you *are* the titular head of your party, candidate or no candidate, and you owe it to the American people . . . to clarify the fact that *the future of our country is at stake in this election.* . . . I would rather see you go down to defeat for the nomination rather than fail to carry out a mission only you can fulfill. . . ." Another supportive voice was that of his old wartime associate George Ball. "Many people are waiting hopefully for you to speak out on the major issues and give some direction to a party that runs the risk of becoming badly confused and divided," Ball informed him in March 1960. He recommended that Stevenson refrain from endorsing any other candidate and expressed hope that a forthcoming speech by Stevenson at the University of Virginia would be "as sharp and clear as possible," and not "have the ring of a commencement address. If it does, there will be vast disappointment since . . . people are yearning for your leadership. . . ." Eleanor Roosevelt (whom Stevenson admired perhaps more than any other living person) also favored his nomination in 1960.[41]

Stevenson seldom needed much encouragement to "speak out" against the Republicans. As Ball recommended, on April 12 he used the Founder's Day address at the University of Virginia to launch an attack on the Eisenhower administration. "We are entering a decade of great decisions affecting our nation, our civilization, and our very survival as human beings," he asserted. "And one of the first of these decisions will be to select leadership that will help us fully understand our choices and our dangers. . . ." For years he had tried to call attention to what seemed to him "the real issues of our time"—the nuclear-arms race, the dynamic character of the Soviet challenge to free society, the "revolution of rising expectations" in the underdeveloped nations, the alleged failure of the Republicans to tell Americans "the truth" about all these matters. By 1960 Stevenson was convinced, as he told one correspondent, that a "whirlwind . . . will surely come before long." He thought he detected the first rumble of the approaching storm in May, when the crash of an American plane in the Soviet Union reverberated around the world, shattered hopes for a relaxation of cold war tensions, and revived his presidential aspirations.[42]

On 5 May 1960, Premier Nikita Khrushchev disclosed that a high-altitude American aircraft had been shot down inside the Soviet Union. The next day the United States said that one of its weather research planes had strayed off course. On May 7 Khrushchev announced that the plane contained photo espionage equipment and that the pilot had admitted being on a CIA-sponsored reconnaissance mission. The United States then acknowledged that such U-2 flights had been conducted over the Soviet Union for several years. At a press conference on May 11, morever, President Eisenhower took personal responsibility for these espionage missions. Just five days later a big-power summit conference was scheduled to open in Paris, but Krushchev demanded that Eisenhower must first punish those responsible for the flights and promise never to resume them. The President refused this "ultimatum," and the summit conference broke up, taking with it any hope for progress toward controlling nuclear armaments.[43]

In a public statement on May 16, Stevenson said that "this whole fiasco discloses the painfully precarious state of our relations, and uneasiness in the world. . . . I hoped from the bottom of my heart that we would reach agreement on stopping nuclear tests at this long awaited meeting." Addressing a Cook County Democratic gathering in Chicago a few days later, he charged that the Eisenhower administration had "played into Khrushchev's hands" by its handling of the affair. "Premier Khrushchev wrecked this conference. . . . But we handed [him] the crowbar and sledge-hammer," Stevenson declared. "We cannot sweep this whole sorry mess under the rug in the name of national unity. . . . Too much is at stake. . . . For in this age, unprecedented in human history, all of us, Americans and Russians alike, have one common enemy . . . the danger of war." "I am glad you approved of my sharp reaction to our summit performance," he wrote to Eugene Rostow (yet another of his wartime acquaintances). "I was fearful that if we sat mute and all rallied round it would appear abroad that even the opposition was unaware and uncritical." He exclaimed to Gerald Johnson, "I can hardly believe that we have suffered this self-imposed blow at this time."[44]

Stevenson's forceful public reaction to the U-2 affair aroused fresh support for him as a presidential possibility. The *Progressive* praised him for daring to "risk the charge of appeasement" in order to express "some tough truths" about American foreign policy. The *St. Louis Post-Dispatch* endorsed him; so did the *New York Post, Newsday* (Alicia Patterson's paper), the *Sacramento Bee,* and the *Nation.* It was his last hurrah, however, because he had steadfastly refused for months to do anything to expedite the slim possibility that he might

be nominated. On the contrary, he had told many potential supporters that he was not interested. "Thank God, I don't have to worry
about these things [presidential politics] any more!" (to Chester
Bowles, October 21, 1959); "I would like your advice—on how *not* to
get nominated! I know when I have had enough" (to Arthur Schlesinger, November 2, 1959); "I have never expected to be nominated
again since 1956 and have done everything short of refusing a
nomination to avoid it—including leaving the country for long
stretches" (to Agnes Meyer, March 10, 1960); "I dread the thought of
ever having to go through the ordeal again" (to Vincent Sheean, April
27, 1960); "I find it hard to understand why people are expecting me
to make a 'decision'. . . . I have said repeatedly that I would not seek
the nomination, and I won't" (to Dore Schary, May 6, 1960); "I won't
be party to any 'stop K[ennedy] movements' " (to Newton Minow,
May 31, 1960); "I must . . . say that I am anxious about your reaction
to my statement that 'I am not a candidate.' Obviously this is what I
had to say, because it is true . . ." (to Eleanor Roosevelt, June 13,
1960).[45]

Despite all his disclaimers, Stevenson would have run in 1960 had
the Democratic National Convention drafted him as it had in 1952.
His law partner Willard Wirtz insisted that Stevenson wanted the
nomination "*very* much." "I know all the reports and impressions to
the contrary. Those reports are wrong," Wirtz emphasized. Early in
June, Stevenson admitted to Thomas Finletter's wife," I will accept a
draft—yes—who wouldn't or couldn't!" But 1960 was not 1952. The
situation was totally different. Then, there were no other viable
candidates in sight. Now, John F. Kennedy came to the convention
with the nomination almost in hand—although he was worried about
Stevenson lurking in the bushes. Then, Stevenson was a fresh new
face in national politics. Now he looked a little shopworn compared
to the glamorous young aspirant from Massachusetts. There is something at once noble and pathetic about Stevenson's attitude toward
the nomination in the final weeks before the convention. On one
hand, he refused to jump into the race at the last minute, knowing
full well that it would contradict all his public statements since 1956
and tarnish his image. On the other hand, he was obviously waiting
in the wings, the perennial "available man," longing for one last shot
at the White House if Kennedy stumbled on the path to the nomination.[46]

For several months James E. Doyle, a Wisconsin Democratic leader, had been working behind the scenes for Stevenson's nomination. Besides Doyle's efforts, other "draft" movements sprouted in the early months of 1960. Stevenson kept all these supporters at arm's length and refused to give them any direct encouragement, but—as Newton Minow has admitted—"we knew what Jim Doyle was doing. The Governor [Stevenson] helped get money for it. . . . Often the Gov. played dumb and innocent when he really knew all about something. In 1960 he kept saying that he didn't want to run—but he was interested." Stevenson mentioned Doyle's efforts with approval in a letter to Agnes Meyer in March 1960. In the meantime, some of the liberal intellectuals, including Schlesinger and John Kenneth Galbraith, who had worked for Stevenson in the past were support-ing Kennedy. After a meeting with Kennedy in June, Schlesinger wrote Stevenson: "K[ennedy] said he regarded the position of en-dorsement that Ken [Galbraith] and I had taken as conclusive evi-dence that you weren't engaged in stop-Kennedy activities." But Schlesinger also assured Stevenson that he had told Kennedy, "You could do him great and probably decisive harm by raising your little finger." At the same time Schlesinger noted in his personal journal: "I have come . . . to the private conclusion that I would rather have K[ennedy] as President than S[tevenson]. S . . . has been away from power too long; he gives me an odd sense of unreality . . . in contrast K gives a sense of cool, measured, intelligent concern with action and power." Having failed to reach the New America on the Stevenson express, the liberal intellectuals had elected to hitch a ride on the Kennedy bandwagon.[47]

The desertion of his old supporters irritated Stevenson. "I find myself getting more provoked by the feeling I get from the Kennedy camp that I should do this or that if I expect any consideration [for a good job] later," he complained to Schlesinger on June 7. ". . . I have always felt in a way responsible for Jack's recent political progress. . . . I wanted him, as you know, to be my vice presidential candidate in 1956. . . . As a result of the convention in 1956 he had a quickly earned national reputation . . . and I have conscientiously kept out of his way since so as not to impede or embarrass his progress. . . ." Stevenson's pride was showing through, and a touch of resentment and jealousy as well.[48]

"I really haven't tried to follow the delegate count," he told Agnes Meyer shortly before the Democrats convened in Los Angeles, ". . . although I have a feeling that our young friend [JFK] may get enough delegates lined up to make it on the first ballot. I really don't care and find strength in the fact that I don't seem to care." He said he was "afraid this will make you angry," but told her that "it gives me a confidence about what I say and do." At the convention, however, Stevenson weakened in his resolve under the entreaties of Eleanor Roosevelt, Mike Monroney, and a few other loyalists. He even made a last-minute bid for delegate support, but when he asked Richard Daley whether there was any backing for him in the Illinois delegation, Daley told him there was none; the delegation was solid for Kennedy. The Cook County organization, which had enabled Stevenson to get into politics in 1947 and helped him to win the nomination in 1952 and 1956, no longer felt he was a viable candidate. On the first ballot Kennedy received 806 votes and the nomination. It was the end of the "Stevenson era" in the Democratic party. He put the best possible face on the outcome and insisted that he felt no regret. "I was determined to stand aside because I thought it impertinent to seek a third nomination," he wrote John Kenneth Galbraith after the convention. But he added, "It never occurred to me that anyone would doubt that I was available if wanted." "I still reproach myself for not having been firmer with you about the third nomination," Agnes Meyer wrote him in September. ". . . you yourself said to me, 'Had I wanted it, I could have taken it away from him'—meaning Kennedy. . . . But you made things just as *hard* for your devoted followers as possible—and now you *regret* it and I do too."[49]

Stevenson's interest in the 1960 nomination demonstrates the continuing allure that presidential politics had for him. He was also deeply concerned over the ramifications of a victory by Richard Nixon in November, yet twice burned at the polls and all too aware of the enormous stress of a national campaign, he could not bring himself to solicit for his party's highest award a third time. In fact, even had Kennedy not won the nomination on the first ballot, it is by no means certain that the convention would have turned to Stevenson, but that is unquestionably what he hoped would happen. In the fall he campaigned vigorously for the Democratic ticket, hoping to be named secretary of state in return for his efforts. When Kennedy narrowly defeated Nixon, Stevenson anticipated happier days for himself and the country after eight years of Republican rule. He was to be disappointed on both counts.

His last years, 1961–1965, were not his best. Denied the position he wanted, Stevenson wound up as U.S. ambassador to the United

Nations, where he was reduced to the role of routineer, an executor of policies made by others. He was busier than ever, but much of the work was mechanical in nature. It was also exhausting. Now sixty-one years old, he began to show signs of age; friends worried about his health. His life was filled with an endless stream of meetings, speeches, receptions, and cocktail parties, at one of which someone found him sitting alone, staring morosely at his shoes. "This job has been a terrible drill," he admitted in a candid interview in 1965. ". . . you take on the coloration of your country . . . and you become predictable." Time was passing. So were some of his friends. Alicia Patterson died in 1963. "It seems unthinkable that she is gone," he wrote to Jane Dick, "and I, for one, will have a hard time reconciling myself to life without the comforting assurance that she would always be there when needed."[50]

Stevenson had a close relationship in this period with Marietta Tree (Mrs. Ronald Tree), whom he had known for years and for whom he arranged a position at the UN. (He also found a job for Jane Dick; he was always loyal to his friends.) His letters to Marietta Tree are strikingly similar to those he once earlier wrote to Alicia Patterson— full of complaints, lonely, introspective, affectionate, mingling personal and public matters. " 'The person who can face both life and love with confidence and courage—and give himself the sheer joy of giving—is sure to find joy and contentment. For loving *is* living.' It sounds well—and is, no doubt, but my trouble seems to be that 'life' is so dependent on love" (Christmas, 1961). "Most of one's life it is impossible to say what is really true! And then—but it is rare—the pulse of feeling stirs again—the heart lies plain—and what we mean we say, and what we would we know!" (undated, 1963). "This morning we go hunting at—2°—but the sun is bright and the snow and moon so white. The ghost, and the creak at the top of the stair,— is always there" (December 1963). "There is much to do here—I can't figure out what happens to my days—there's seldom time to go out to lunch; I'm home weary every night; the mail and papers pile up hopelessly . . ." (July, 1964). "Things are bad in the UN: trouble everywhere . . . worse than any time since Cuba" (August 1964). "Tues. night—1:00 A.M. . . . I struggled to get thru the day's office work and then a speech for this morning in Atlantic City to the Rotary International. . . . The speech worked—why I don't know—and I flew back to N.Y., again content . . . but with that uncomfortable questioning—what am I doing all this for—for me? . . . for who? . . .

and I'm alone—at last—with nothing except these blank pages and a speech to do for Arkansas day after tomorrow—and no time tomorrow" (May 1965).[51]

Work had been Stevenson's salvation since he moved into the Illinois governor's mansion in 1949. His duties at the United Nations, however, afforded him relatively little sense of satisfaction, particularly when controversial United States policies in Cuba, the Dominican Republic, and Vietnam jeopardized his reputation as a man of integrity. He survived the fallout from the abortive Cuban invasion in 1961, but in retrospect it would have been better for his reputation if he had resigned his position soon thereafter. Instead he persevered, remaining in his post after President Kennedy's assassination at Lyndon Johnson's insistence. As he told an interviewer, "It's easy to reconcile a sense of duty with this job." Besides, he had nothing else to do.[52]

When fighting erupted between leftists and rightists in the Dominican Republic in the spring of 1965, President Johnson ordered U.S. Marines into the country to restore order and prevent a Communist coup—a move all too reminiscent of the days of gunboat diplomacy in the Caribbean. After Stevenson's death, the political commentator David Schoenbrun reported that at a dinner party in Paris Stevenson had strongly criticized the Dominican intervention. According to Schoenbrun, Stevenson termed the intervention "a massive blunder," questioned whether there was a geniune danger of a Communist takeover, and said that defending the intervention at the UN "took many years off my life." Averell Harriman, who was also present on this occasion, subsequently challenged Schoenbrun's account of the conversation. Others said that if Schoenbrun had known Stevenson better he would have realized that these remarks were typical Stevenson grumblings. There are hints in Stevenson's correspondence, however, that he was in fact unhappy about the Dominican operation. Meanwhile the Johnson administration was escalating the war in Vietnam, and also escalating Stevenson's problems at the UN.[53].

In June 1965 a delegation of writers opposed to American policy in Vietnam came to Stevenson's office and called on him to resign as an expression of disagreement with the Johnson administration. He listened politely to their arguments but declined to do as they demanded. Afterward, Nat Hentoff, one of the group, described his impression of the meeting. "At the end, he said—and I did not feel it to be rhetoric—'You honor me by coming. I do not have the chance often these days to have this kind of dialogue.' Leaving, I was depressed. I had the sense of his impotence—and the sense of his knowing and caring deeply, hopelessly, about the impotence. He could not resign. That was not the way he played the game. And because he could not—would not—change the rules, he had been trapped by them."[54]

While some of his critics wanted Stevenson to resign in order to publicize their antiwar views, others were sincerely concerned about his reputation. They thought the government was using him for its own purposes. In a sense they were correct, as a message sent by the United States Consul General in Canada to the State Department reveals. The consul general reported that a speech made by Stevenson in Toronto in May 1965 "had tangible plus values both in exposing the limited numbers and the lack of sophistication of the local protestors against U.S. policies . . . and in exposing the . . . humane viewpoint of Ambassador Stevenson to a large audience. . . ."[55]

One of Stevenson's greatest admirers in the journalistic ranks was Murray Kempton. On the eve of the 1960 election, for example, Kempton wrote in the *New York Post:* "Let us never forget that if a light still rises above this dreary land, it is because for so long and lonely a time this man [AES] held it up." On June 2, 1965, concerned about the course of events in Southeast Asia, Kempton sent Stevenson a letter pointing out that the U.S. government repeatedly had lied to the American public. "At such moments, the private man is our one essential resource," Kempton emphasized. "I know that I am asking you to do one more messy and exhausting thing; but could you come out here and lead us?"[56]

No, he could not—for many reasons. Stevenson was a company man, relentlessly loyal to his government. To resign as a gesture of public disagreement was unthinkable to him. He also may have hoped that by remaining at his post he could encourage the administration to move toward a negotiated settlement in Vietnam. In fact, he had been involved in efforts to arrange secret talks between the United States and North Vietnam through the auspices of the UN Secretary General (see Chapter 3). Moreover, despite his difficulties at the UN, it is doubtful that he truly relished the prospect of returning to his home in Illinois and that "ever-threatening solitude." Stevenson believed that through public service he could exercise a measure of influence on his times. For him, to be active in public affairs was to be directly engaged with the momentous issues of the day. He could imagine no higher calling. "I'd like to think that I'm a high-minded, decent, enlightened citizen who's . . . trying to play his part in his generation," he remarked to an interviewer in 1956, ". . . and move on to my place in the shadows having left behind something better than I found." By 1965 the stakes seemed greater to him than ever. He told friends that he had nightmares about a nuclear holocaust, portending the end of civilization. It was no time to retire to the wings.[57]

If he missed his cue to exit and lingered onstage too long, if his lines began to sound a little hollow, it was because the public role that had sustained him for so long could not be lightly set aside. When the curtain abruptly fell on July 14, 1965, as he walked along a London street with Marietta Tree, he was still in harness, playing his part to the end.

2

"A SEAMLESS MORAL GARMENT": THE AMERICAN POLITICAL SYSTEM

On his last night in office in 1953, the outgoing governor of Illinois took time to reply personally to one of the countless letters he had received from the general public after the 1952 presidential election. This particular admirer reassured him that he had been right in trying to "talk sense" to the electorate during the campaign. Now, as his term dwindled down to its last hours, Adlai Stevenson wrote, "You need have no doubt that your remarkable letter of November 6 was read. I have read it very carefully, and it has enriched me. 'Telling the people' *is* a 'mind-beating and manbreaking' task. But somehow I think they know, not always at the same time, but *in* time—usually." This was the faith that sustained him through a political career that contained its full share of disappointments and frustrations.[1]

1

From the 1930s to 1965, amid depression, world war, and cold war, Adlai Stevenson retained a deep faith in the American political system. Neither the traumatic historical events of his time nor his personal setbacks in politics shook his belief in the democratic process, because it rested on an ultimate confidence in the American people themselves. "You can't be contemptuous or tricky or condescending with the electorate," he emphasized to the journalist Joseph Alsop in 1952. "You've got to assume that the people of the state are just as able as you are to understand what's best for the state. . . . If this weren't true, life wouldn't be worth living." "If I were to attempt to put my political philosophy into a single phrase," he declared in a speech during the 1956 presidential campaign, "it would be this: Trust the people. Trust their good sense, their decency, their faith. Trust them with the facts. Trust them with the great decisions." Several weeks after the 1956 election, he gratefully responded to a letter from Murray Kempton. "How I wish I had your facility for expressing what I think! 'The Republicans ask us to trust a man' Adlai Stevenson asks us to trust ourselves.' Yes, that was the whole thing. . . ."[2]

Since every politician dutifully praises "the people" as the source of all wisdom and virtue (especially at election time), it would be easy to dismiss Stevenson's remarks as mere rhetoric. In this instance, however, the rhetoric, however unoriginal, even banal, rested upon a genuine philosophy of democratic government. He adhered to that philosophy even though he knew perfectly well that neither the knowledge nor interest of the public approximated his idea of a healthy democratic system. "I think the trouble is that the people are far away, and getting farther away, from government," he commented to Gerald Johnson in 1958. Stevenson saw the separation of the people from their government as potentially fatal to the system simply because in his view the system *was* the people, and vice versa. Whenever ignorance, apathy, immorality, or cynicism gains a foothold among the public, the entire system becomes infected. For, as he saw it, democratic government can be no better than its parts, i.e., the politically involved segment of the population. He explained his thinking in numerous speeches, perhaps most forcefully in a nationally broadcast address during the 1952 campaign.

What is the lesson of history and of all human experience? What is the primary law of life? You struggle and you survive—you fail to struggle and you perish. . . . Nature is indifferent to the survival of the human species, including Americans. . . .

I repeat, then, that the task is yours. Yours is a democracy. Its government cannot be stronger or more tough-minded than its people. It cannot be more inflexibly committed to the task than they. It cannot be wiser than the people. As citizens of this democracy you are the rulers and the ruled—the law-givers and the law-abiders—the beginning and the end. Democracy is a high privilege. But it is also a heavy responsibility whose shadow stalks you although you may never walk in the sun.[3]

As these solemn remarks indicate, Stevenson conceived of government as essentially a moral process; he assumed, moreover, that morality was not a divisible commodity. Speaking to the Association of American Law Schools in 1953, he explained that "the morality of government is, like the law, a seamless garment, and it cannot be rent in one small place without endangering the whole fabric." Ten years later he drew the same analogy in a speech to the convocation of the Center for Democratic Institutions, contending that "equality before the law and at the ballot box are only strands in the seamless robe in which all our liberties are woven together. Carelessly unravel one, and the robe itself may come apart." The seamless moral garment was an apt metaphor to describe Stevenson's sense of democracy as a holistic process, which the citizenry and their leaders have a mutual responsibility to uphold.[4]

If Stevenson was a visionary concerning what government should be, he was realistic about what government usually is—imperfect, prone to inefficiency and corruption at all levels. He could hardly deny this fact after having spent four years (1949–1952) trying to run the government of the state of Illinois, a task calculated to break the will of any idealist. Yet he emerged from the experience not in despair but even more convinced that democracy could work if the people wanted it to work. In a radio address to the citizens of Illinois in January 1953, he said that he wished there were time to talk in more detail about "our successes and our failures . . . what I've learned that's so and what I've learned that isn't so," about "politics and patronage, law enforcement, gambling, corruption, about human beings, the good and the evil, and all the things that have made these four relentless years here in Springfield the best in my life." In private life, however, he struck a less buoyant tone in a letter to Eric Sevareid. "As for the [presidential] campaign, I have no regrets, and my conscience is comfortable," he wrote in late November 1952. "My only misery is the State of Illinois and the apparent disinterest of masses of good people in preserving what we so painfully accomplished here."[5]

Stevenson had campaigned for governor in 1948 as a classic "good government" advocate. It was scarcely a unique approach to running for public office, but it proved to be particularly effective in Illinois in 1948 because Stevenson had the advantage of being an "outsider" who was not identified with the political machines in Chicago or East St. Louis. He also benefited from some well-publicized scandals in the administration of the incumbent governor, Dwight H. Green. Over and over again as he traveled around the state, Stevenson promised the voters he would bring a new era to state government if they sent him to Springfield. In these speeches, many of which he drafted himself, he set forth the essential elements of his democratic philosophy: all citizens are responsible for the moral health of government; people should not expect government to be better than they are; maintaining good government is an unending, often unrewarding process, and so on. "It's our job as candidates and as the organized leaders of our party to tell the people the naked truth," he told the Democratic party state convention in May 1948. "Then it is up to them to decide whether . . . they want honest, wholesome government in Illinois, or are content to languish four more years in political bondage to political brigands." At the same time he was mastering the fine art of partisan politics. He spoke of "the political pirates in the State House," "gang government in Springfield," "Governor Green, the errand boy for the Chicago Tribune," "the Green machine," etc. Stevenson was always a more ardent party man than many of his admirers, who thought of him as a politician who transcended politics, realized. He argued endlessly that the Democrats had a better claim than the Republicans to the support of "the people." Such conventional partisanship would hardly merit attention were it not for the fact that Stevenson placed so much emphasis on the moral dimension of politics; consequently each time he departed from his exalted standards it was an implicit commentary on the viability of his political philosophy.[6]

He was aware of the problem. He once admitted that the "business of talking both to a partisan Democratic group and beyond them to the people, presents obvious difficulties which I lamely resolve by trying to do both." Stevenson claimed he would "far prefer to talk to America as an American and forget the partisan aspect. . . ." But as titular head of his party in the 1950s he had to make frequent attacks on the Republicans, and he generally seemed to have little trouble rationalizing his partisanship. Most politicians do not have to worry about such considerations. Stevenson did, because his philosophy was predicated on the concept of indivisible morality throughout the political process.[7]

Having captured the state house by pillorying the Green administration for its alleged moral lapses, Stevenson worried about scandals throughout his own administration. Like all reformers who come to power, he found that it was easier to denounce corruption in others' houses than to prevent it in his own. Overall his record was good in this respect. He ordered raids on illegal gambling activities, placed the corruption-infested state police on a personnel merit system, and took a personal interest in virtually every department of state government. He also made some excellent administrative appointments.[8]

Two of his appointees became tainted by controversy. Jim Mulroy, a former newspaperman who had helped to manage Stevenson's gubernatorial campaign and then became his executive secretary, bought stock in a Chicago race track linked to organized crime. Mulroy was probably guilty of nothing more than bad judgment, but Stevenson accepted his resignation. Another scandal involved Charles W. Wray, whom Stevenson had personally hired to be superintendent of foods and drugs. Wray was implicated—though later acquitted—in a syndicate conspiracy to make hamburger out of horsemeat. Carl McGowan, who was serving as administrative assistant for legislative relations in Springfield, remembers a depressed Stevenson asking him, "My God, if Wray goes sour, I don't know, what can you depend on?"[9]

The Mulroy and Wray cases, combined with other experiences in Springfield, simply reinforced Stevenson's conviction that good government depends on good people. He emphasized this point in his farewell address in 1953: "Government—local, state and federal—is not something separate and apart; if it is to be good it must share the attitudes and the competence of the best in our society as a whole." He sounded almost Calvinistic when he talked about his fundamental concept. "No approach to the problem of corruption in government is good enough," he warned in a 1952 campaign speech, "if it ignores the deeper problem of corruption in men—of men."[10]

The frustrations he encountered in trying to attack organized gambling in Illinois severely tested Stevenson's moral philosophy of government. He sent the state police on numerous raids against gambling houses, but he knew he was only chipping away at the tip of the iceberg. The real culprit was not the gambling operators, he told the American Bar Association in 1950; it was the prevailing attitude of "public indifference and cynicism." "In ordering these raids, I did not feel the joyful exhilaration of a knight in shining armor tilting with the forces of darkness. I felt more like a mourner at a wake. For something had died in Illinois—at least temporarily." Discussing the gambling issue on another occasion, he pointed out that a private citizen who played a slot machine in his country club was in no position to "insist that his elected officers enforce the law in the corner saloon."[11]

The moral lesson posed by the gambling problem had profound ramifications in Stevenson's thinking. During the early 1950s he repeatedly alluded to the concept of indivisible morality, invariably arriving at the same conclusion: Do not expect more from government than you expect from yourself. Addressing the graduating seniors at Princeton University—his alma mater—in 1954, he asked them, "How many respectable citizens do you know who protest loudly about the lawlessness and venality but don't hesitate to fix a traffic ticket?" He told the young Princetonians that "it is the duty of an educated man in America today to work actively to put good men into public office—and to defend them there against abuse and the ugly inclination we as human beings have to believe the worst."[12]

Stevenson's preoccupation with the moral element in democratic government—indeed, the moralistic tone of his entire political philosophy—was hardly unique in American political thought. It owed a great deal to the reform rhetoric of the Progressive era in the first decades of the twentieth century. After investigating various city governments in the United States around the turn of the century, Lincoln Steffens had concluded that corrupt urban administrations fed upon a corrupt or apathetic citizenry. When Stevenson made a statement like "behind every bribe taker in government is a bribe giver," he was speaking firmly in the moralistic Progressive tradition. He shared many features of the Progressives' view of democratic government: its moral basis; the correlation that should exist between the people's attitudes and those of their leaders; the faith that the electoral process can produce good candidates; the belief that such persons when elected to office can—with the help of professional administrators—make government more efficient, more responsive to the public will, more reflective of the general interest.[13]

Also Stevenson's political thought, like that of the Progressives, has in retrospect a rather innocent quality. He appeared to underestimate the strength of the forces that can corrupt government no matter how many "good men" hold office. Perhaps this weakness stemmed from the fact that much of his thinking about the political system was based on his experience as a state governor. The government of Illinois, for all the challenges and frustrations it presented, was not the federal government. It could not compare in size or complexity with the vast federal bureaucracy that had developed since the Progressive era. His comment to Gerald Johnson in 1958 indicated a growing concern about the distance between the people and their government. Even if he were alive today, however, Stevenson would undoubtedly still insist that no one has a right to complain about "the government" if they are unwilling to get involved at the local level. Harry Truman proclaimed, "The buck stops here"; Stevenson thought it should *start* "down there," in neighborhoods, towns, and counties—and ultimately in the character of the citizenry. He felt that there were virtually no limits to the ramifications of this truth. In October 1949, with the cold war under way, he spoke to the Inland Daily Press Association in Chicago. He told the audience that there was a connection between the problems of the world and those he faced in Springfield. "In a world plunged into a bitter war of ideas, the words and platitudes uttered by you or me today or our statesmen tomorrow won't have much effect," he declared. "But what happens in each of those 155,000 [local] governments in this country . . . will have its effect, because the quality of democratic government can never be better than the average of its parts."[14]

2

Since Stevenson's political philosophy was predicated on confidence in "the people," one must try to account for the origins of his faith. Where and how did he acquire it?

There is no simple answer. How does anyone come to believe in something? Usually it is the result of experience. So it was with Stevenson. One can identify some of the factors that presumably contributed to his democratic faith: the pervasiveness of the Lincoln legend in Illinois, the Stevenson family's acute awareness of its own history of public service, the patriotic tone of education in Stevenson's youth, and a habit of mind that enabled him to see the best in people rather than the worst. Concerning Lincoln, for whom he had a lifelong reverence, he once asked, "How did Lincoln arrive at this deep faith in mankind? Because he was one of them . . . he *knew* the people good and bad, ridiculous and sublime, and he believed there was more good than bad in most of them."[15]

Lincoln knew the people at first hand, but for many years the same could not be said of Stevenson. Basically Stevenson lived in an insulated milieu until he was in his forties. Growing up in a wealthy family with a rather domineering mother, spending summers abroad or at resorts for the rich, going off to Choate School at the age of sixteen and thence to Princeton, studying law at Harvard and Northwestern, entering the Sidley law firm on LaSalle Street and socializing with Chicago's North Shore set, was not the Lincolnian path to greatness. Stevenson's service in the Navy Department and the State Department during World War II and his work at the United Nations immediately after the war vastly enlarged his horizons, but even in those years (1941–1947) most of his personal associations were with other men of social privilege whom he encountered as diplomats and administrators. He remained distant from the common people.

Part of his reluctance to run for governor after the war stemmed from his unfamiliarity with the grass-roots problems of Illinois. Stevenson rightly felt his experience best qualified him to run for the U.S. Senate. He undertook the gubernatorial campaign reluctantly, but wound up regarding it as an invaluable educational experience. As he traveled around Illinois during 1948, the phrase "the people" took on a new meaning for him. It was transformed from an abstract noun into farmers, factory workers, housewives, Kiwanis members, labor leaders, coal miners, schoolteachers, teen-agers, retired persons, et al. The gubernatorial campaign exposed Stevenson to ordinary Americans whom he had never before known. In subsequent national campaigns he met millions more of them, but his first political odyssey in Illinois left a lasting impact on him. One day during the campaign he scribbled a note to his old friend Jane Dick: "It's Sunday morning. I'm in an automobile driving from Danville where we spoke last night to Decatur to resume this fantastic ordeal. . . . It's been an amazing experience, and I've come to wonder how anyone can presume to talk about 'America' until he has done some campaigning." To Carl McGowan he wrote that the campaign was "a wonderful experience, and I am mortified to confess that I knew but little of Illinois before." He told another correspondent that the campaign had been "an awful ordeal, but a great experience."[16]

On September 15, 1948, as summer slowly gave way to autumn

across the Illinois prairie, Stevenson spoke in his hometown of Bloomington. He lavishly praised the town and its people, declaring that they represented "the ideals of the Middle West—neighborliness, friendliness, belief in the Republic, trust in the democratic principle. . . ." He said that any honors he had received "have come because some people thought I had certain qualities that are not uncommon here in Bloomington." He spoke eloquently about the town's influence on his democratic ideals.

> I have Bloomington to thank for the most important lesson I have ever learned: that in quiet places, reason abounds; that in quiet people there is vision and purpose; that many things are revealed to the humble that are hidden from the great.
>
> And my home town taught me that good government and good citizenship are one and the same, that good individuals made a good town—and that nothing else does. I learned that good communities make a good state and nothing else can.
>
> I hope and pray I can remember the great truths that seem so obvious in Bloomington, but so obscure in other places.[17]

The speech revealed much about the man. After barnstorming all over the state, getting an education in practical politics, he came home to make an idealistic statement about democracy. There is no way to know whether his youth in Bloomington had actually had the impact on Stevenson that he claimed it had. His remarks are hard to square with the cool observation of a lifelong Bloomington resident that Stevenson "never was fully accepted here until he was brought back for burial." The fact remains, however, that Stevenson obviously wanted to believe that Bloomington was the sort of town that he claimed it was. More important, he wanted to believe that American democracy in general rested on the kind of moral structure that he ascribed to Bloomington. He had an endless capacity to blur—or in his mind to reconcile—those things that are and those that ought to be.[18]

"It has been a difficult and at the same time fascinating experience," he said of the governorship in a letter to a navy friend after having spent sixteen months in Springfield. "Rubbing shoulders day and night with the hard realities of politics and human nature at this level is quite a different thing from my prior experience. . . . Indeed, I am afraid that one of the by-products is a rapidly diminishing ambition for much more of it. . . . But I am really not a pessimist as you know!" He was anything but a pessimist—and far more ambitious than he indicated. Stevenson eventually gained a world-wide audience for his philosophy. But he never revealed his tendency to merge ideality and reality more dramatically than he did in his hometown on an early autumn evening in 1948.[19]

3

As Stevenson moved into national politics in the 1950s, he often talked about what he called "the reputation of government." In other words, did people believe what the government told them? Did they trust the government? Would they come to its support and do its bidding in a crisis? In his speech to the Association of American Law Schools in December 1953, he explained that by "the reputation of the government" he meant something more than the need to guard against traditional forms of corruption. He felt there was a deeper dimension to the problem, "a quality . . . I can only call justness—the meeting of the popular expectation that government is a protector of the basic equities. . . ." In "these trying times," he warned, "no government . . . can afford to jeopardize" the loyalty of its citizenry.[20]

Underscoring these comments was the political atmosphere of the early fifties, a period of exceptional rancor between the political parties. Ever since Franklin D. Roosevelt came to power in 1932, conservatives had been frustrated by what they saw as the sellout of traditional American principles by the New Dealers. The bipartisan unity tenuously created during World War II, coupled with the government's retreat from reform during the war, temporarily muted the critics' voices. After the war, however, a series of events played into their hands: the Yalta controversy and the Soviet Union's gains in Eastern Europe, the Alger Hiss case, and other sensational espionage revelations, the triumph of Communism in China, the first Soviet atomic bomb, the frustrating war in Korea. These developments, compressed into the few years between 1945 and the early 1950s, bewildered Americans who had hoped for a period of relaxation after fifteen years of depression and global war. Instead they were confronted with one crisis after another, while Republicans anxious to gain power and Democrats fearful of losing it polluted the air with acrimonious charges and countercharges. What was really on trial was the New Deal tradition, as the Republican senator Hugh Butler's soliloquy on Secretary of State Dean Acheson made clear: "I watch his smart-aleck manner and his British clothes and that New Dealism, ever-lasting New Dealism, in everything he says and does, and I want to shout, 'Get out! Get out! You stand for everything that has been wrong with the United States for years!'" Then, in 1952, the Democrats nominated Stevenson for President, a man who had served in the New Deal, who had helped to establish the United Nations, who had defended President Truman's policies in Korea— although he never mentioned Dean Acheson by name during the campaign—and who had testified in behalf of the reputation of Alger Hiss. Despite all these handicaps, Stevenson proposed to rise above the din and "talk sense" to the American people. "Unless the great political parties and their spokesmen assume responsibility for educating and guiding the people with constant candor," he asked, "how can we be sure that majority rule will meet the test of these searching times?"[21]

There was much to recommend the strategy of talking sense. Stevenson genuinely believed in it, and anyway he was temperamentally unable to deliver to the opposition Truman-style "hell." But he was grossly mistaken if he believed he could remain aloof from the intense party warfare of the day. Soon he was up to his ears in partisan wrangling. The Republicans portrayed him as a radical New Dealer, while he stigmatized them as reactionaries who would repeal every piece of progressive legislation on the books if they got the chance. He claimed that the so-called Old Guard had taken over the Eisenhower campaign, lock, stock, and barrel. He interpreted the reconciliation between the Eisenhower supporters and those of Senator Robert Taft (spokesman for the conservative Republicans who was denied the nomination) as "a sordid triumph of expediency over principle," and claimed that it proved that the "forces of reaction" were "once more unconquerable" within the Republican ranks. Deliberately invoking memories of the Great Depression, he asserted that the Republicans offered "no evidence that they have departed from their 1930 patented formula of 'let boom and let bust.' " Was this how he proposed to talk sense to the voters? Stevenson was on firmer ground when he denounced right-wing extremists' insinuations that traitors had infiltrated the highest levels of government. For example, Senator William E. Jenner (R.-Indiana) called General George C. Marshall a "front man for traitors," and Senator Joseph R. McCarthy (R.-Wisconsin) said Marshall was part of a conspiracy "so immense

. . . as to dwarf any previous such venture in the history of man." Stevenson charged that the tactics of these "salesmen of confusion" were "unworthy of people aspiring to leadership. . . ." After the campaign General Marshall told Stevenson, "Your political speeches reached a new high in statesmanship."[22]

Both sides were guilty of verbal excesses in this period. Frustration over their long exile from power encouraged some Republicans to make irresponsible accusations against the Democrats. Senator Taft exemplified the tendency. He had long enjoyed a reputation for exceptional integrity and attachment to principle. Unfortunately, even Taft succumbed to the partisan pressures of the early fifties. Although he privately expressed doubts about the accusations of Senator Joseph McCarthy, Taft defended him in public as "a fighting marine who risked his life to preserve the liberties of the United States." This was utter nonsense, as was Taft's assertion that the "greatest Kremlin asset in our history has been the pro-Communist group in the State Department who surrendered to every demand of Russia at Yalta and Potsdam, and promoted at every opportunity the Communist cause in China. . . ." Some of Eisenhower's speeches in 1952 conveyed the same message, most notably an address he gave in Senator McCarthy's home state of Wisconsin, when Eisenhower charged that the "very brains" of certain unspecified men in government had been "confused by the opiate" of Communism. What did this mean? "It meant—in its most ugly triumph—treason itself," Eisenhower declared. His opponent's apparent acceptance of the "twenty years of treason" thesis prompted Stevenson to charge that Eisenhower had capitulated to the right-wingers. Amid this frenzied political atmosphere, no candidate could fulfill the hope that Stevenson had expressed to his friend Archibald MacLeish at the outset of the campaign: "I hope and pray I can keep my debate up on a level of honor, dignity and public enlightenment. . . ."[23]

All things considered, Stevenson probably did the best he could under the circumstances. Some of his campaign speeches, such as the remarks he made to the national convention of the American Legion about the excesses of the superpatriots, and his address at the University of Wisconsin on the meaning of freedom, did him real credit. He told the American Legion that there was "no justification for indiscriminate attacks" on public schoolteachers. He warned against "intolerance and public irresponsibility cloaked in the shining armor of rectitude and righteousness." He affirmed that "sinister threats to the Bill of Rights, to freedom of the mind," were often disguised as patriotism, whereas true patriotism was "an inner light in which freedom lives and in which a man can draw the breath of self-respect." In Madison, Stevenson talked about "the Wisconsin idea—the faith in the free mind and in the application of reason to government." After reiterating his own firm opposition to Communism ("the first casualty of the communist regime is the free mind"), he condemned those Americans "who, in the name of anti-communism, would assail the community of freedom itself." Suggesting that Senator McCarthy's search for traitors was contrary to the so-called Wisconsin idea, Stevenson concluded, "I hope that the time will never come in America . . . when the voice of the accuser stills every other voice in the land. . . . We will not be stampeded into the dark night of tyranny." Such affirmations, delivered at a time when fear and acrimony pervaded American politics, perhaps constitute Stevenson's finest hour.[24]

The Republican victory in 1952 calmed the political waters somewhat but scarcely ushered in an era of good feeling. Senator Joseph McCarthy continued his rampage against government; his demagogic search for traitors in high places recognized no party boundaries, and he quickly became an embarrassment to the Republicans. Meanwhile the displaced Democrats found life in the political wilderness no more rewarding than the Republicans had in previous years. Stevenson established the main party line against the Eisenhower administration in a Democratic fund-raising speech in New York in February 1953. His basic theme was that the administration was dominated by big businessmen and did not represent the common citizen. "There is always the possibility that the successor of the New Deal will turn out . . . to be the Big Deal," he quipped, "while the New Dealers have all left Washington to make way for the car dealers—I hasten to say that I do not believe the story that the general welfare has become a subsidiary of General Motors." It was a good line, but it ignored the fact that most of the New Dealers had left Washington years before. Warning his audience against the Republicans' alleged "tendency to mistake the particular interest for the general interest," Stevenson affirmed that his own party was the party "of all the people" and therefore had a better claim to their support than did Eisenhower and company. It was the classic American reform theme, utilized over the years by Jeffersonians, Jacksonians, Wilsonian progressives, and New Dealers. Like his political forebears, Stevenson maintained that government should represent the general interest rather than special interests. But his only suggestion for achieving this goal was to throw the Republicans out and bring the Democrats in.[25]

His explanation of the difference between the parties was obviously unoriginal and simplistic. Who would seriously maintain that either party has a monopoly on special interests? Stevenson's comments on the Republicans were standard operating procedure for a Democrat. But his intensified partisanship after 1952 disappointed some persons who had been captivated by his rhetoric in the presidential campaign. Gradually the view spread that he was "just another politician," which in a sense was true. He was a party loyalist who wanted to believe that politics could transcend partisanship in some unspecified fashion. When he came down to earth and began to attack the Eisenhower administration in conventional political terms, he did seem to be "just another politician." Stevenson did not change dramatically after the 1952 campaign, but in trying to help the Democrats regain power, he was victimized by a vision of politics that no politician could live up to.

During the 1954 midterm elections Stevenson toured the country, stumping for Democratic candidates. It was another bitter campaign, filled with stale echoes of the acrimonious allegations of recent years. Obscured by the haze of rhetorical warfare was the fact that both parties had come to a grudging agreement on the essential items of public policy: anti-Communism abroad, the post–New Deal mixture of free enterprise and governmental regulation at home. Perhaps this underlying consensus helps explain why much of the political rhetoric of the period focused on personalities and such nonissues as the "loss" of China and Communists in Washington.

At any rate, the 1954 elections produced anything but reasoned public debate. Stevenson, now more comfortable amid the din of name-calling, gave as good as he got, but he knew it was not an uplifting brand of politics. Speaking at a party rally in New York in late October, he made a plea for rationality: "Our nation faces grim years ahead—years which will test to the utmost our resolution, our will, and our faith. . . . After a responsible campaign our country and our people would have been better equipped to cope with these realities than we were three months ago. Instead, the nation has been recklessly torn apart in the search for votes. . . ." He cautioned that the "challenge is not just to win elections," but to generate "hard and healthy debate" over the "legitimate differences in policy" between the two parties. But he could not separate these worthy sentiments from his corresponding conviction that the Republicans were largely to blame for what he termed "the progressive degeneration of this campaign." "We have observed with sorrow the effect that the pressures of partisanship and political ambition have had on the top leaders of the Republican party. . . . No reputation, no record, no name—no Democrat in short—has been immune from savage or sly attack on his integrity, his good sense, his very loyalty. . . . Those who seek victory at this price can be rebuked in only one way—that is, at the polls."[26]

These comments reveal Stevenson's dilemma. Ardently convinced that political debate should follow the high road, he could only account for the fact that it often wound up on the low road by blaming the opposite party. Like the preacher uncovered in the whorehouse, his protests were qualified by circumstances. Yet he himself had chosen those circumstances. He could have retired from politics after 1952 and concentrated on his law practice, or perhaps lectured on politics in a university. But Stevenson was an activist, a politician to the core. He relished the excitement of combat, preferred the battlefield to the lectern, thrived on the hunt for votes. It was becoming, more than he would admit even to his closest confidants, his life. This meant that try as he might—and he did try—his political ideals and the political realities which he had to confront would become hopelessly confused.

More than any other single subject or person, Stevenson's political rivalry with Richard Nixon caused him to compromise his ideals. The two men could hardly have been more different in background, psychology, temperament, and political orientation. If they shared anything in common it was ambition, and even this characteristic was manifested by each in very different ways. To Nixon, Stevenson must have seemed the epitome of the patrician in politics, condescending and arrogant; to Stevenson, Nixon appeared the quintessential politician on the make, intemperate and unscrupulous. Between Whittier, California, and Bloomington, Illinois, there was an unbridgeable gulf—Ragged Dick versus the Squire of the Manor. They came from different worlds. The potential for mutual mistrust was inherent in their characters; the intense partisan political atmosphere in which they each sought power brought it to a boil.

Stevenson's sister, Elizabeth Ives, has said that her brother's dislike for Nixon dated from Nixon's tactics during his 1950 Senate campaign against Helen Gahagan Douglas in California. The first public exchanges between Nixon and Stevenson occurred during the 1952 presidential campaign over the subject of Alger Hiss. Stevenson had known Hiss in 1933 and again in the years 1945-1947 when both were working for the federal government. In 1948 Hiss was accused by Whittaker Chambers before the House Un-American Activities Committee of having been a Communist agent in the 1930s; Chambers, himself a self-avowed former Communist, claimed that Hiss had given him classified government documents. In 1949 lawyers for Hiss asked Stevenson to respond to a deposition concerning their client. Stevenson testified that Hiss's character had been "good" at the time as far as he knew. During the 1952 campaign Nixon, who had gained political capital for helping to "break the Hiss case" as a member of the House Un-American Activities Committee, used the 1949 deposition against Stevenson. "Mr. Stevenson has not only testified for Alger Hiss," Nixon charged, "but he has never made a forthright statement deploring the damage that Hiss and others like him did to America because of the politics and comfort they received from the Truman Administration and its predecessors."[27]

Stevenson replied to Nixon in a speech in Cleveland, attempting not only to answer Nixon but also to head off the impact of a forthcoming speech by Senator McCarthy. Stevenson defended his deposition as an act of voluntary compliance with a court order; he said that lawyers had a particularly pressing obligation to cooperate with the courts; he reviewed the specific language which he had used in the deposition. Then he turned to the subject of Nixon, whom he called "the brash and patronizing young man who aspires to the Vice Presidency." "He has criticized my judgment. I hope and pray that his standards of 'judgment' never prevail in our courts, or our public life at any level, let alone in exalted positions of respect and responsibility."[28]

Relations between Stevenson and Nixon further deteriorated in the 1954 elections when Nixon, like Stevenson, delivered numerous speeches for his party's congressional aspirants. He linked Stevenson with so-called Left Wing Democrats whose foreign policies had "resulted in the loss of 600,000,000 people to the Communists" since World War II. He implied the Democrats had Communist support, saying that the Communist party was "determined to conduct its program within the Democratic party. . . ." Speaking in Milwaukee, Stevenson observed, "It looks as though the Great Crusade [of

Eisenhower] under the leadership of Snow White [Nixon] is going to end up . . . on the elevated note of subversion, perversion and denunciation." He called such tactics "McCarthyism in a white collar." Nixon later termed this statement a "typically snide and snobbish innuendo toward the millions of Americans who work in our shops and factories." He indirectly referred to the Hiss deposition again by declaring that "working people have a much keener and clearer understanding of the threat of communism at home than Mr. Stevenson has displayed during his public career."[29]

Perhaps Nixon had been the aggressor in their earlier exchanges, but Stevenson—whose advisers told him there were votes to be gained in talking tougher—took the offensive in the 1956 campaign. By this time, both in public and in private, he associated Nixon's name with the worst in political ethics. For example, he told the New York Liberal party that he had no desire "to deprecate the Vice President's new personality," but said that he hoped that the "new Nixon" would see fit to repudiate "the irresponsible, vindictive and malicious words so often spoken by the imposter who has been using his name all these years." In Los Angeles he questioned whether many people were ready to accept Nixon as "the Little Lord Fauntleroy" of the Republican party: "They wonder if he doesn't yearn for his old tar bucket and his brush." Turning to the subject of the Vice-President's alleged "adaptability," Stevenson declared:

> What "adaptable" means here is that this man has no standard of truth but convenience and no standard of morality except what will serve his interest in an election. . . . Our nation stands at a fork in the political road. In one direction lies a land of slander and scare; the land of sly innuendo, the poison pen, the anonymous phone call and hustling, pushing, shoving; the land of smash and grab and anything to win.
> This is Nixonland.
> But I say to you that it is not America.[30]

On the eve of the election, facing another probable defeat, Stevenson let out all the stops in a nationally broadcast speech from Boston. Calling attention to President Eisenhower's poor health (the heart attack in 1955 and subsequent intestinal surgery in 1956), he asserted that "every piece of scientific evidence" indicated that the President might not survive another term. "I say frankly, as a citizen more than as a candidate, that I recoil at the prospect of Mr. Nixon as custodian of this nation's future, as guardian of the hydrogen bomb, as representative of America in the world, as Commander-in-Chief of the United States armed forces," Stevenson stressed. "Distasteful as it is, this is the truth, the central truth, about the most fateful decision the American people have to make tomorrow."[31]

Stevenson's attacks on Nixon can be explained by Nixon's provocations in the past, electoral pressures, and a genuine conviction that Nixon's character was flawed. But they cannot be justified; they did Stevenson no credit and they probably hurt him at the polls. Willard Wirtz, Stevenson's friend and law partner who was closely associated with the 1956 campaign, claims that Stevenson regretted some of the rough language he used against Nixon in the campaign, particularly during a speech in Flint, Michigan. "Stevenson did not want to give that speech," Wirtz insists. "He . . . despised what he had done in Flint. . . ."[32]

Stevenson preferred to think that political criticism, rather than degenerating into the kind of name-calling that characterized politics generally in this period, could have a positive function. Ideally, he felt, criticism should help educate the electorate by giving the people clear choices between contrasting positions on the issues. When political parties performed their job of criticism in a responsible fashion, he thought, they strengthened the system. The "very goodness of a society can best be measured by the freedom with which men may honestly speak their minds," he said. "For, paradoxical though it may seem, free criticism can flourish only in a society where mutual trust is strong." In practice, however, Stevenson placed limits on the boundaries of free criticism. He termed criticism "irresponsible" if it raised questions about the credibility of the government; presumably he felt that the times were too perilous for any doubts to be entertained in the public's mind on that score.[33]

Stevenson was not alone in assuming that the credibility of the American government should lie beyond reproach. The cold war restricted the range of political discussion in the 1950s; it precluded free, unhampered public debate. Virtually no "responsible" public figure doubted that the Soviet menace required a measure of conformity and consensus; it was time to rally round the flag. Anyone who ventured beyond the pale, who tried to pose fundamental questions about American purposes or values, was certain to be denounced by liberals and conservatives alike. Indeed, it was partly because Senator Joseph McCarthy refused to observe the limits of permissible political behavior that almost everyone in politics eventually denounced or abandoned him. McCarthy was, of course, an unscrupulous demagogue. But it is also clear in retrospect that he posed a threat to the whole cold war consensus that all "responsible" politicians, liberals as well as conservatives, embraced like drowning men clinging to a frail line. Unsure whether to sink or swim, they wasted their energies fighting over the portion of line available to them. As Joseph Wood Krutch observed at the end of the decade, the problem during the 1950s was that "too few who believed that they were asking fundamental questions went on to ask others still more fundamental"; they continued instead "to accept premises which made searching inquiry impossible."[34]

To his credit Stevenson occasionally rose above this suffocating consensus, but more often than not he accepted its premises. Thus he could say in 1954, "The fact is that we are Americans, first, last, and always, and may the day never come when the things that divide us seem more important than the things that unite us." He was ultimately a man of his times, and the political culture of the times restricted the permissible range of political criticism. That is partly why he deplored the Republicans' charges of "twenty years of treason," of the "loss" of China, etc. Such accusations seemed "irresponsible" to him because they called into question the credibility of the government. To Stevenson, this was not playing the game within the rules. Yet after the Republicans took over in 1953, he seems to have had no trouble rationalizing his attacks on the Eisenhower administration—presumably, these came under the heading of "responsible" criticism.[35]

The Korean War furnishes the best example of Stevenson's selective view of political criticism. He believed that the war was an unpleasant but necessary means of reaffirming American determination to stop Communist aggression and of demonstrating the credibility of the United Nations. Writing in *Foreign Affairs* (April 1952), he warned: "To call Korea 'Truman's war' distorts the entire historical significance of our prompt response through the United Nations to the cynical Communist challenge to the whole concept of collective peace and security. . . . We are trying to use force not only to frustrate our immediate antagonists in the hills of Korea but to preserve world peace." Throughout the 1952 campaign and afterward, he continued to defend this proposition, while suggesting that anyone who questioned it was a political opportunist. In December 1953, a few months after a truce had been negotiated to end the fighting, he declared that public support of the war furnished "the supreme example in my lifetime of the essential need for mutual trust and confidence between the ordinary citizen and his government." He insisted that the American people had believed President Truman in 1950 when he said the national interest required sending troops to Korea. "Our people, with that sixth sense which is at once the inner grace and outward shield of democracy, seemed to know, however imperfectly, they were being summoned to the highest kind of duty," Stevenson asserted. He claimed that they had responded to Truman's call "because of their respect for the right of government to ask the ultimate in sacrifice for aims judged by government to be necessary."[36]

A dozen years later, as United States ambassador to the United Nations, Stevenson found himself defending another undeclared war in Asia. But by then the popular climate of opinion had changed. Some tough questions were being asked about matters that had been implicitly deemed off limits once the cold war began—such as the relationship of undeclared Asian wars to American security. Official rationales, which formerly had been more or less accepted, were beginning to be more critically evaluated and found wanting. As President Lyndon Johnson's administration plunged deeper into Vietnam in the name of maintaining American credibility, its own credibility at home steadily eroded. "Public confidence in the integrity of the government is indispensable to faith in democracy," Stevenson had proclaimed in 1952. "When we lose faith in the system, we have lost faith in everything we fight and stand for." This was precisely what began to happen in the sixties. Public trust in government gradually yielded to a pervasive public skepticism and cynicism. College-educated young people were the first to express this attitude as they felt the Vietnam war impinge on their lives; in the seventies it began to infect larger segments of the population in the wake of the Watergate affair.[37]

Stevenson died just as the process of alienation was beginning. In his last years he seemed unable to appreciate how his public identification with the Johnson administration's policies in Southeast Asia contributed to the very erosion of public trust he deemed indispensable to democracy. It is a depressing story, because no other politician had spoken more eloquently about the need to maintain the people's faith in government. Somehow, what happened to him at the United Nations—like his failure in 1954 and 1956 to maintain his own high standards of political debate—is more than a judgment on Stevenson's personal shortcomings. It is a sobering commentary on the corruptive capacity of the political system itself.

5

Although Stevenson stressed the importance of a politician explaining the issues to the electorate, he failed to communicate with the majority of voters in the 1952 and 1956 presidential elections. Even had he not run against an inordinately popular war hero and father figure, his inability to convey his ideas to the voters would have made it hard for him to win a national election. The complicated syntax of his speeches, his wry, self-deprecating humor and cultivated manner, won over millions of Americans, to be sure; but millions more could not understand him—or did not bother to try— and voted for Ike. In his second bid for the White House, Stevenson reluctantly tried to play the game in more conventional ways, donning silly hats, kissing babies, even posing with a Democratic donkey. These tactics were not his natural style, and he was clearly uncomfortable with them. Many voters undoubtedly concluded that he was not interested in the common people. They were wrong. John Bartlow Martin has recalled a day in 1956 when Stevenson left the campaign bus in California and began playing croquet with some old men in a park. It was as if "he had come all the way to California for the sole purpose of playing croquet," Martin remarked.[38]

Such incidents revealed the human warmth and genuine curiosity about people that lay behind Stevenson's outer reserve and endeared him to those who knew him best. But most voters never saw this side of the candidate. To them it seemed that this cultured, reserved man lacked some essential quality of experience with life as they knew it. Franklin Roosevelt, a political genius, overcame his patrician background to win the trust—and love—of the masses. Stevenson never found the key to their hearts—perhaps because he tried to hard to reach their minds. Roosevelt reveled in traditional campaign hoopla; Stevenson endured it. Once while he was seeking votes in Florida, for instance, someone thrust a stuffed alligator into Stevenson's hands. Instead of accepting the trophy with a grateful grin, he rasped, "For Christ's sake, what's this?" He had little patience with the carnival side of politics; therefore, he concluded, perhaps too readily, that it was only a sideshow which detracted from a candidate's effort to educate the electorate. But, for better or worse, Americans always have sought to be entertained at political rallies at least as much as they have wanted to be informed. Stevenson was not unaware of this fact, but he knew his limitations. As he told Gerald Johnson in 1955, "I can campaign only one way, I fear—my way.[39]

Stevenson particularly disliked having to battle Estes Kefauver—a master showman on the stump—through the state presidential primaries in 1956. He felt that the primaries overexposed him, sapped his energy, forced him to use up his ideas prior to the main performance against Eisenhower in the fall. "I do not enjoy it, and what makes me uncomfortable and depressed is the rapid sequence of total surprises with no preparation or previous indoctrination," he confided to Agnes Meyer from California during a political tour of the Golden State in February 1956. "I have never enjoyed slapstick politics or extemporaneous speaking and that seems to be all that is contemplated." He told her that it was "an awkward posture for me to be in when I am trying to be the 'responsible' candidate and most of the pressures are either for irresponsibility or banality." Perhaps he would have felt differently about the primaries had he been in Kefauver's position—disliked by the party powers and forced to pursue the nomination via the primary route. He finally turned back the colorful Tennesseean's challenge, but he feared that in winning the battle he might have lost the war. After capturing the California primary in June, he expressed relief in a letter to Barry Bingham, a Louisville, Kentucky, newspaper publisher, who was a good friend and political supporter, that "this insane endurance contest is over." "There are so many things to do," he lamented, "and I had so much wanted to approach the [National Democratic] Convention fully prepared this time. . . ." He felt that the primaries were one of the most irrational aspects of the American political system, because they detracted from time better spent boning up on the issues.[40]

In fact, "the issues" became almost an obsession with Stevenson as time passed, and no issue seemed more fundamental to him than the way in which the United States exercised its power in the world. The "power, for good or evil, of this American political organization," he had reminded the Princeton seniors in 1954, "is virtually beyond measurement. The decisions which it makes . . . the leadership which it provides on moral as well as material questions, all appear likely to determine the fate of the modern world." Six years later, in the 1960 presidential campaign, he reiterated his holistic philosophy in a speech to the New York Liberal party. "I don't know, frankly, whether this nation as we know it would survive another motionless administration. . . . But I do know it cannot survive indifference of its citizens." It was the same message he had tried to convey a dozen years earlier to the people of Illinois about their responsibility to maintain the health of state government. Only by now he had expanded the scope of the idea to national and global dimensions.[41]

Stevenson's holistic moral philosophy also conditioned his views of the presidency. That was what led him to tell the Democratic convention in 1952, "I would not seek your nomination . . . because the burdens of that office stagger the imagination." In 1955, as pressure mounted on him to announce his candidacy for 1956, he protested to his confidante Agnes Meyer, who was urging him to run again, "You must not think badly of me for 'not wanting it'. . . . To know the proper measure of this task precludes anybody but the lightheaded or ruthless from 'wanting it,' it seems to me." In 1960 he repeated his view to another correspondent shortly before the Democratic National Convention: "First, let me say that I have always felt that in theory, at least, no one should seek his party's nomination for the Presidency; that an office so exalted and so impossible to fill should be beyond the presumptions or conceits of men; that to assert one's competence, indeed superior qualifications, for that office was a reflection of excessive ambition and arrogance and presumption. But this attitude, I know, is not common, and I have no doubt that men will always seek the office instead of the office seeking the man."[42]

Of course, these sentiments did not prevent Stevenson from wanting to be President. He would have accepted the nomination in 1960 if he had been offered it. He was always less than candid about his ambition, but it is true that he had a genuine reverence for the presidency. His sensitivity to the far-reaching consequences of presidential power prevented him from pursuing the office with the singleness of purpose demanded by the political system. This reluctance was one of the basic differences between Stevenson and such other politicians as Kennedy, Nixon, et al. On the one hand, he was in awe of the moral ramifications of the presidency; on the other hand, he was fascinated by its potential for bettering men's lives. His ambivalent view of the presidency helped create Stevenson's "indecisive" reputation and alienated politicians who were less troubled by such considerations. Whether his acute awareness of the moral implications of power would have made Stevenson a weak President is an intriguing but unanswerable question. His admirers will always think he would have made a great leader; his critics will always doubt it. One can only say with confidence that he would have been an extraordinarily conscientious Chief Executive.

Whatever reservations he entertained about himself or the presidency, Stevenson had no trouble criticizing his opponent's performance in the office. For eight years (1953–1960) he repeatedly charged that Eisenhower was failing to lead the country. On all the principal issues of the day, foreign and domestic, he thought Eisenhower's policies misconceived and his leadership inept. Both publicly and privately he declared that the President had failed to give the country moral leadership. Looking ahead to the 1956 election, Stevenson told Agnes Meyer in 1955, "Actually, superficially, there seems to be little at stake, but I think we realize that mediocrity, materialism, social indifference and repulsive showmanship cannot be forever disguised by wholesome smiles, golf clubs and a Bible firmly clutched beneath the right arm if seldom read. . . ." In his speeches he charged that Eisenhower had "abdicated responsibility" in all areas of public policy: regulation of big business, conservation of natural resources, civil rights, civil liberties, and foreign affairs. In the American system of government, Stevenson believed, only the President can transcend the demands of special interests because nominally the President alone represents all the people. Only the President could arouse in the people "the common impulse to honor in our daily lives the principles we proclaim to all the world," Stevenson told a Democratic rally in 1956. "For his office is the repository of moral authority as well as legal. . . ."[43]

Few historians would deny that the record of the Eisenhower administration furnished fuel for criticism, although it was by no means as lackluster as Stevenson and the Democrats claimed. Whatever one thinks of Eisenhower's leadership, the relevant question here is; Did Stevenson, as opposition spokesman, provide substantial alternatives to the administration's policies? At the outset of the Eisenhower years he proclaimed, "A political party which cannot in defeat make itself an effective instrument of larger national purposes is without significance in the future political life of the country. . . . For the party out of power, principle—and not patronage—must inevitably be the only solvent." In private he spoke more cautiously, admitting to Eric Sevareid that the "problem of 'party leadership' has infinite difficulties and hazards. . . ." This was particularly true with respect to the Democratic party in the fifties, deeply divided between Northern and Western liberals and Southern conservatives. Under these circumstances, Stevenson soon learned that it was far easier to talk about moral leadership than to exercise it. What seemed moral to one Democrat might seem immoral to another. Compounding Stevenson's problems was the fact that the "titular head" of an opposition party in the American political system really has nothing but a title. Stevenson had no office, no staff, no funds, no institution-alized means of communicating either with other party leaders or with the public at large. The Democrats who had these means at their disposal were the congressional leaders, Lyndon Johnson and Sam Rayburn, who often disagreed with Stevenson's views. Stevenson was also frustrated by the proclivity of most newspapers and news magazines to support the administration; by comparison, he com-plained, his criticisms received scant attention from the press. In 1957 he angrily charged that the "immunity [of the Eisenhower adminis-tration] from criticism from a large segment of the press, combined with massive and skillful use of propaganda and advertising," had brought about "a crisis in the honest political communication on which an informed electorate must depend." Denying that he was "troubled by the fact that most of our press lords are partisan Republicans," he claimed that he was primarily concerned "with the deterioration of democracy, when self-criticism withers, debate dries up, and power over the mass mind is concentrated in a few hands."[44]

There is no doubt that Stevenson labored under some distinct handicaps. How well did he manage to overcome them? Analysis of three issues—school desegregation, the Indochina crises of 1954, and the hydrogen-bomb testing controversy in 1956—provides mixed reviews of his leadership as titular head of the loyal opposition.

On May 17, 1954, the United States Supreme Court, in the case of *Brown* v. *Board of Education of Topeka,* reversed the doctrine of "sepa-rate but equal" facilities in public education set forth by the Court in 1896 (*Plessy* v. *Ferguson*). Now the Court unanimously held that separate educational facilities were "inherently unequal" and ordered gradual desegregation. No prominent American political figure could deny the profound implications of this ruling. One looks in vain among Stevenson's letters at the time, however, for any reference to the case. Two years later, amid the presidential campaign, he charged that Eisenhower by failing to put the moral force of the presidency behind the Court's decision had in effect underminded it. But what did Stevenson himself say about the ruling when it was first announced? In fact, he made no public comment at all for ten days. On May 27, he issued a cautious statement clearly aimed at appeasing the South. Stressing that the South had been invited by the Court to participate in drafting means of implementing school desegregation, he said, "The rest of the country should extend the hand of fellowship, of patience, understanding, and assistance to the South . . . because it isn't just a Southern problem, it's a national problem, even as the Constitution governs us all." Segregation and racism were indeed national problems, but Stevenson's statement was less than a ringing endorsement of the decision of the highest court in the land.[45]

Stevenson was titular head of a party partly composed of Southern segregationists. The only states he managed to win in 1952 were in the South. He was fearful of saying anything on the subject of race relations that might undermine the position of Southern moderates who were opposed to the rabid segregationists. Moderates like Harry Ashmore of the *Arkansas Gazette* frequently advised Stevenson to proceed with caution on the race question. In August 1956, for instance, Ashmore told him that "in the long run their [i.e., the segregationists] cause is hopeless, but . . . pressure only tends to harden the mood." Stevenson had emphasized to Eleanor Roosevelt a few weeks before he received Ashmore's letter that "I would gladly withdraw from this political contest if it would . . . save the party from breaking up and enthroning the white extremists in the South or losing the Northern cities and thus the election." It is hard not to sympathize with Stevenson here. He wanted to do the right thing, but the political situation in which he found himself was extremely delicate. One might, argue, however, that he paid too much attention to politics and not enough to conscience. For some people the civil rights issue was a moral question if ever there was one. From their perspective, Stevenson was too timid in his approach. They felt a greater moral imperative was at stake. Stevenson looked at the situation in a different light; he was fearful of inadvertently playing into the hands of the segregationists and thereby making matters worse. Still, it is unfortunate that in 1956 Stevenson chose to moralize about President Eisenhower's failure to provide leadership in civil rights. It was a cheap shot, the politics of expediency. In retrospect, neither Eisenhower nor Stevenson fully appreciated the moral or political urgency of the race issue. They were both gradualists.[46]

The reverberations of the *Brown* ruling shook the country just as another political tremor centered in Southeast Asia was dissipating. For several weeks in the spring of 1954, the Viet Minh, a coalition of nationalist and Communist forces, had besieged Dienbienphu, the principal French military stronghold in Indochina. The siege of Dienbienphu marked the final stage of a long war in Indochina led by Ho Chi Minh against French colonialism. Despite large amounts of American aid, the French were on the ropes. What would the Eisenhower administration do? The options available to the President included the use of American air power, even ground troops. Eisenhower decided not to bail out the French, and Dienbienphu surrendered to the Viet Minh early in May.

Two years later Stevenson raised the Indochina issue in the presidential campaign. He charged that "the free world suffered a severe defeat in Asia and lost a rich country and more than ten million people in Indochina" while Eisenhower played golf, presumably unconcerned about the crisis in Indochina. But how would Stevenson have responded? He was stoutly opposed to colonialism, but he was also a fervent anti-Communist. What would he have seen as the correct moral course of action when the French appealed for American support? Would Stevenson have chosen to intervene in Southeast Asia, as Presidents Kennedy and Johnson did in later years? When he was asked in April 1954 for a public statement on the Dienbienphu situation, he replied that his comments would have to be "exceedingly temperate because of my want of information on the subject at this time." He lamely remarked that he felt Secretary of State John Foster Dulles's recent call for "united action" in Indochina was an attempt "to reassure the French and the rest of the world of our interest in this situation."[47]

Perhaps Stevenson was just trying to avoid playing politics with the issue. Nevertheless, his response was inadequate. If he felt that the United States had an obligation to help the French, he should have said so, or if he thought that the best American policy was to stay out of the debacle, he should have said so. His failure to say anything of substance suggests that he knew that the Indochina situation did not lend itself to simple moral judgments. (He had acknowledged as much when he visited the region in 1953.) Later, however, as with the civil rights issue, he did not hesitate to criticize the Southeast Asia policies of the Eisenhower administration. Addressing a Democratic gathering in Nebraska during the 1954 congressional campaign, he charged that the United States had lost

"12,000,000 to 13,000,000 people" to Communism in Indochina. Then he urged the Democrats not to exploit the issue as the Republicans had exploited the "loss" of Eastern Europe and China! If Stevenson meant for the audience to take his warning seriously, why did he raise the subject at all? Such tactics resembled those he denounced when they were employed by the Republicans, as did his repeated assertion in the 1956 campaign that the free world had "lost" half of Indochina to Communism. Was he implying that Eisenhower should have tried to save Dienbienphu? Or did he mean that the principal American mistake lay in having supported the French all along? If he meant the latter (as he probably did), he conveniently overlooked the fact that Eisenhower's Democratic predecessors in the White House had begun the policy of aiding the French. Partisanship not only prevailed here over Stevenson's ideal of responsible political criticism; it also blunted the political impact of his critique of the administration's faltering foreign policies, because he failed to present a clear alternative.[48]

Greater consistency between his theory and his practice of political leadership characterized Stevenson's discussion of the hydrogen bomb in the 1956 campaign. Nothing troubled him more than the specter of nuclear holocaust. He confided to several people that it gave him nightmares. Fear of Armageddon underlay his commitment to the United Nations and to the effort to create a more rational framework for the conduct of international relations. To propose that the United States stop atmospheric tests of nuclear weapons, he hoped, would elicit substantive debate on the idea and contribute to public enlightenment on an issue of fundamental importance to all people. Instead, he was denounced by the Republicans and members of his own party for raising the subject.

Stevenson first suggested that the United States "give prompt and earnest consideration to stopping further tests of the hydrogen bomb" in an address to the American Society of Newspaper Editors in April 1956. He said such a step "would reflect our determination never to plunge the world into nuclear holocaust. . . ." He had discussed the problem of radioactive fallout with Atomic Energy Commissioner Thomas Murray in the winter of 1956. He also corresponded with Benjamin Cohen (Roosevelt's old adviser who was knowledgeable about nuclear matters), Thomas Finletter, George Kennan, and others. The speech for the Society of Newspaper Editors evolved through several drafts written by Benjamin Cohen, Arthur

Schlesinger, Jr., and Willard Wirtz. It was apparently Stevenson himself, however, who chose to suggest that the United States act unilaterally to halt atmospheric testing. At a press conference on April 25, 1956, Eisenhower disparaged Stevenson's proposal, thereby establishing the basic attitude of his administration toward the issue for the duration of the campaign. Stevenson reiterated his proposal in the fall. When Eisenhower again dismissed it as a "theatrical gesture," he protested, "I was shocked when Mr. Eisenhower . . . brushed off my suggestion as a theatrical gesture. I don't believe it was worthy of the President of the United States. I have never questioned his sincerity on . . . the matter of permanent peace—and I do not think he should have questioned mine." On October 6 Eisenhower issued a special statement on the issue which repeated the administration's position that it would be unwise to halt the tests without "proper safeguards."[49]

Meanwhile Vice-President Nixon and other prominent Republicans assailed Stevenson. Thomas E. Dewey called him "a spokesman for the proposals of Moscow." Senator Karl Mundt of South Dakota said he had done "a disservice" to the country. Attorney General Herbert Brownell predicted Stevenson's suggestion would "bring joy to the hearts of those who expect to wipe out the free nations one by one." Nixon declared it raised "grave doubts as to whether [Stevenson] has the judgment, the responsibility, and the temperament to lead the United States and the free world. . . ." Despite this torrent of abuse, Stevenson continued to argue that there was nothing to be lost from suspending the tests. He maintained that Eisenhower's talk about safeguards was irrelevant because the United States could effectively monitor tests by other nations anywhere on the globe. He also stressed the lethal consequences of radiation poisoning, an aspect of the subject he had not emphasized earlier. In a nationally broadcast speech on the H-bomb in mid-October, he said, "With every explosion of a super bomb huge quantities of radioactive materials are pumped into the air currents of the world . . . later to fall to earth as dust or in rain. This radioactive 'fallout' carries something called Strontium 90, which is the most dreadful poison in the world. . . . In sufficient concentration it can cause bone cancer and dangerously affect the reproductive processes." He added, "I do not wish to be an alarmist and I am not asserting that the present levels of radioactivity are dangerous. Scientists do not know exactly how dangerous the threat is. But they know the threat will increase if we go on testing."

He concluded, "People everywhere are waiting for the United States to take once more the leadership for peace and civilization. We must regain the moral respect we once had and which our stubborn, self-righteous rigidity has nearly lost."[50]

It was all to no avail. The administration had managed to put Stevenson on the defensive: by having to deny that his idea posed any threat to national security, he in effect conceded the advantage to the Republicans. He was bitter over what had happened. "I am sure I am on solid ground here," he wrote to the British economist Barbara Ward in October. He told her the administration was "unspeakably culpable in its failure to do anything whatever about the most terrible thing on earth." He insisted to another British friend, "On the H-bomb tests I must stick to my position and convictions and what I am sure is fundamentally sympathetic to our people." When President Kennedy signed a test-ban treaty with the Soviet Union in 1963, Stevenson wryly remarked to John Steinbeck, who had written to him recalling his efforts in 1956, "I am comforted that someone hasn't forgotten, now that the bandwagon is so crowded. I guess seven years is too far to be ahead of history!"[51]

Robert A. Divine has argued that Stevenson's H-bomb proposal, along with his concurrent assertion that the military draft be terminated, was a major political mistake because he was challenging the administration in the area of national security, where Eisenhower was "virtually impregnable." Moreover, Divine notes, Eisenhower genuinely thought that the H-bomb and draft issues were purely political ploys on the part of the Democrats, and this conviction gave the President's "denunciations an air of outraged sincerity." The nuclear-testing question was indeed a complicated one, ill suited to the demands of a modern political campaign for brevity and simplicity. Still, Stevenson's decision to raise the issue and his perseverance on the subject gave credence to his assertions about the proper function of political criticism, and the responsibility of politicians to attempt to educate the electorate.[52]

Is it feasible for candidates even to delve into complicated questions in a modern political campaign? Stevenson thought the preservation of democracy depended on their willingness to do so. But his discouraging experience with the nuclear-testing issue in 1956 called into question some of his assumptions about the political process. "I came out of this campaign more than ever convinced that it is all but impossible to make issues during the campaign," he told Dean Acheson in December 1956. "They have to be made first, and the campaign is at best an effort to persuade the voters that one alternative is better than another for their solution." "The campaign is over. I said what I thought needed saying," he complained to Agnes Meyer. "What more could I do? If the people didn't care to listen, or thinkers to agree, or writers to reflect, I cannot feel that I wholly failed in *my* duty."[53]

Stevenson was feeling a little sorry for himself and understandably so. He had been constantly on the move for a solid year, speaking until he was hoarse, shaking hands until his own were swollen, seeking vainly to overtake the popular incumbent President. Now, in a mood of postelection blues, he felt somewhat defensive about his efforts. Nevertheless, his remarks to Acheson and Mrs. Meyer underscored a real concern over what was happening to the electoral process. He told another correspondent that Eisenhower's victory was "more a 'triumph for the age of advertising' than an expression of confidence" in the President. He was wrong in ascribing the outcome wholly to advertising. He never appreciated Eisenhower's genuine popularity with the voters. But Stevenson was right in noting that sophisticated advertising methods had affected the outcome of the election. To him, this development had disturbing implications for democracy.[54]

Stevenson feared that elections were deteriorating into exercises in the manipulation of the electorate. In a speech in St. Louis in 1956, he deplored what he termed the "bread and circuses" approach of the Republicans, claiming that the G.O.P. was out "to sell Eisenhower and Nixon again to a docile, complacent, carefree people all happily chanting 'Peace, Prosperity and Progress—ain't it wonderful!' " The purpose of these tactics, he charged, was "not to excite thought or provoke discussion." Rather, it was "in the finest advertising tradition, to get at our electoral subconscious and persuade us to vote . . . for things as they are." By comparison, he reflected: "How remote this all seems from the classic symbol of American political maturity— the Lincoln-Douglas debates, where, before rapt crowds, the two men hammered out, with all the rational conviction and skill they possessed, the real issues facing a nation in crisis." It was a somewhat idealized depiction of the Lincoln-Douglas exchanges, as well as an obviously partisan perception of the Republican campaign. What disturbed Stevenson, however, is an even greater cause for concern today. As national political managers increasingly rely on advertising methods to "sell" the desired "image" of their candidates, how can the people make an intelligent choice at the polls? An underlying cynicism about the general public suffuses this approach to electoral politics as surely as it characterizes the marketing of consumer goods on television. The fact that several of President Nixon's chief advisers in the White House were drawn from the ranks of the advertising world, and the retention of media consultants by all candidates, indicates how far the process has advanced since Stevenson deplored it in 1956. Granted that his concern would carry more weight had he not equated the use of marketing methods solely with the Republicans, he certainly identified a technique that has become far more sophisticated in the intervening years, one that—whether employed by Democrats or Republicans—seems to assume that how candidates "project" carries more weight with the electorate than what they say. That is exactly what troubled him.[55]

Stevenson was never comfortable with television. He did not like to watch it or to use it in his campaigns. David Halberstam reveals that Stevenson could not watch Nixon's now-celebrated "Checkers speech" in 1952 because he did not have a television set. When Louis G. Cowan, a television producer who later became president of CBS, suggested that Stevenson do some short televised blurbs in 1952, he replied indignantly, "This is the worst thing I've ever heard of. Selling the presidency like cereal. Merchandising the presidency. How can you talk seriously about issues with one-minute spots!" By 1956 Stevenson made a halfhearted effort to utilize the medium, but he remained suspicious of it. Late one night he called Bill Wilson, a television producer from Chicago who had joined the campaign as its TV adviser, and asked him if he could come and fix the set in Stevenson's hotel room! After all, was not Wilson supposed to be the television expert?[56]

If, as Stevenson assumed, democracy depends on an indivisible moral bond between the people and the politicians, one may fairly ask, Where did he think moral leadership came from? Can even the President provide it if the public is indifferent? Stevenson had no answer, but one point is clear: His philosophy was not in tune with the popular mood of the 1950s. About all he could do was rationalize his defeats by insisting the people would eventually awaken from their slumber and energize the political process. "I emphatically share your view about . . . 'What America is and where it is going,' " he wrote to the historian Julian P. Boyd in 1959. "I wish I could say something about this that would be arresting, but I have long since despaired of finding words or the means of public attention. Maybe the time is coming, as you say, when the people will be more receptive."[57]

He had been concerned for years about finding a way to arouse the public, since he assumed that democratic government depends on "public enlightenment and understanding" at the grass roots. "But how do we go about interesting the generally disinterested citizenry in the all-important problems of our states?" he asked a Chicago audience after his first few months as governor of Illinois. "How do we arouse the kind of public concern which brings about effective action in state government?" Here was the critical question—finding the means of arousing the public—which neither four years as chief executive of Illinois nor eight years as titular head of the national Democratic party resolved to Stevenson's satisfaction. In fact, his public career failed to provide conclusive evidence that the public conscience could be more than spasmodically aroused even by the most determined or eloquent leader. "I wish, I wish, I wish I knew how to stir the torpid hearts [of the public]," he lamented to Gerald Johnson in 1957.[58]

Stevenson steadily refused to acknowledge that the effort to do so was inherently futile. To make such an admission would have been to abandon his view of human nature, of politics, of virtually everything. Therefore he could never renounce the faith that he expressed in a letter to Archibald MacLeish at the outset of the 1952 campaign. "I get so sick of the everlasting appeals to the cupidity and prejudice of every group," he complained to MacLeish. "There is something finer in people; they know that they *owe* something too. I should like to try to appeal to their sense of obligation as well as their avarice." Of course, a candidate could win votes "by appealing to passions . . . to self-interest, to fear," he acknowledged in a magazine interview in 1956. "But the best way to win votes is through reason. If I didn't believe that, I couldn't believe in the democratic process."[59]

Stevenson liked to relate an anecdote concerning an incident which supposedly encouraged him to enter politics. Whether the story is literally true is less important than what it reveals about his view of the political process. He claimed that when he was in Italy during World War II he saw a public-opinion poll which stated that seven of ten American parents said they would disapprove if their children

entered politics. Stevenson was appalled; it seemed "curiously incon-
sistent" to him that while people were willing to die for their country
in wartime, they were loath to serve it in peacetime. "Small wonder, I
thought, that our 'politics' is no better, and great wonder that it is as
good as it is." For twenty years he adhered to the holistic theory of
government. As he put it in 1948, representative government "cannot
be wholesome, efficient and healthy at the top and corrupt, cynical
and careless at the bottom."[60]

Stevenson's thinking on these matters exposed him to the charge of
being an idealist. In some respects, he was. To say merely that he was
an idealist, however, leaves unanswered some important questions
about both his philosophy and the political system in general. But
was Stevenson any more of an idealist than those much-acclaimed
"realists" who wrote the United States Constitution? Did they not
create a government whose survival ultimately depended on the
people? Stevenson once noted that Thomas Jefferson's confidence in
the people was "based . . . on a clear, hard-headed realization that
only on such a foundation could 'the last, best hope of earth'
endure." He thought that his view of democratic government rested
on the same basis as that of Jefferson. While he lacked Jefferson's
originality and true philosophical quality of mind, Stevenson was
thinking in the tradition of the enlightenment when he placed the
future of the Republic in the hands of a responsible political leadership, supported by an educated citizenry acting on sound moral
principles. For the democracy he envisioned emphasized people's
obligations as much as their rights. He knew that somewhere along
the way they had to learn, through formal education and practical
experience, the responsibilities of citizenship. He believed it was the
duty of politicians at all times to facilitate the educational process, to
help the people understand the issues in an ever more complicated
world. As he asked Gerald Johnson, "How can a system which
depends on the surveillance of public opinion, on an 'informed
electorate,' be healthy if the people don't know the score—even
approximately?"[61]

"So much of democratic leadership," he insisted, "is just . . . the
maintaining of a oneness between leadership and following." But
how much easier it was to proclaim that ideal than to achieve it!
Meanwhile, Stevenson's partisanship was constantly at odds with his
philosophy. In January 1960, when it appeared probable that his old
rival Nixon would be the Republican nominee for President, he wrote

to Julian P. Boyd: "I suspect you will agree that we have little to look forward to from Nixon but a continuation of the sedatives and half truths which satisfy the majority of people." One might well ask, Are these easily deceived people the same ones upon whom Stevenson thought democracy depended? If so, what does their alleged susceptibility to "sedatives and half truths" suggest about the viability of his philosophy?[62]

Yet despite the constant demands of party politics, despite being twice overwhelmingly rejected by the electorate for the highest office in the political system, Stevenson continued to profess confidence in both the people and the system. Whatever questions it left unresolved, this faith gave his public thought great resilience amid adversity and lasting appeal to those Americans who shared his belief that in a democracy the people "owe something" to the system—and to their own better selves.

3

"STRIVING TOWARD COMMUNITY": INTERNATIONAL RELATIONS AND FOREIGN POLICY

IN THE SPRING of 1954 the United States and the Soviet Union confronted one another as fervent ideological foes, just nine years after American and Russian troops embraced amid the ruins of the Third Reich. In Asia, the Communists controlled China, and the French desperately sought to hold on to their crumbling position in Indochina. In Washington, Secretary of State John Foster Dulles talked ominously of "massive retaliation" against the USSR while Senator McCarthy directed his search for traitors at the U.S. Army itself. Amid this climate of crisis and confusion, Adlai Stevenson, speaking at Harvard University in March 1954, attempted to put the world's troubles in perspective.

"Great movements and forces, springing from deep wells, have converged at this mid-century point," Stevenson declared. He acknowledged that the "mortal contest with world communism" was front and center on the international stage, but he also called attention to "the opaque, moving forms and shadows of a world revolution, of which communism is more the scavenger than the inspiration; a world in transition from an age with which we are familiar to an age shrouded in mist." Americans must learn to deal with this changing world, Stevenson emphasized, "because it seems to me that the historic drama of the twentieth century dwarfs in immensity all our other concerns. . . ." In the atomic era "even the most fanatical faith is likely to balk at self-destruction. . . . Even the most fanatical ambition must adjust itself to demonstrated truth or perish." America's immediate task, therefore, was "to convince the rulers of the other world that they cannot extend their system by force, or by stealth." But its long-term responsibility was to reinvigorate and extend "the moral sentiments of human liberty and human welfare embodied in the Declaration of Independence and the Bill of Rights." For these values, not material wealth or weapons, comprised America's true strength amid the "everlasting struggle between right and wrong" running throughout human history.[1]

These were characteristic Stevenson sentiments: eloquent but vague generalizations, suffused with a strong moral tone and sense of urgency; vigorously anti-Communist but inclined to stress the importance of strengthening democratic values, rather than sheer military force, in the cold war; sensitive to the implications of the post-imperialist age for American foreign policy, but shy on specific recommendations. Stevenson always considered foreign affairs his forte and regarded it as the most important area of public policy. But he never received an opportunity to make foreign policy, either as President or as secretary of state. He was restricted to the role of critic without portfolio in the Eisenhower years, then to that of advocate with portfolio under Presidents Kennedy and Johnson. Nothing in Stevenson's career caused him more disappointment and frustration than his failure to attain a position of authority in foreign affairs, because in this critical field he believed he had something to offer his country and the world.

1

Stevenson evinced interest in foreign affairs as early as the 1920s, when he made several trips abroad, including a visit to the Soviet Union in 1926 that left a lasting impression on him. "After what I saw there, I could never believe, as so many did in the early 1930s, that Soviet Russia's was a good way for any state to go," he recalled years later. "I felt that I had seen at first-hand what Communism really meant, in terms of terror and brutality." Anti-Communism became a staple ingredient in Stevenson's thought. His deep love for his country and his faith in democracy prevented him, even as an impressionable young man in the 1930s, from holding a brief for Communism. He did not understand the allure of Marxist philosophy to many liberals during the Great Depression. Whereas they rediscovered the virtues of the American political system in the forties, Stevenson had remained a believer in it all along. His urbane manner clothed a deep reservoir of nineteenth-century patriotism, an unquestioning confidence in the superiority of American democracy to all competing philosophies and systems. While ideological debates raged in the thirties, Stevenson was quietly establishing a law practice and starting a family. He worked briefly in Washington for two New Deal agencies, but his letters in those years seldom referred to public affairs, either foreign or domestic. Indeed, from his correspondence alone, one would hardly know that the country was locked in the worst depression in its history.[2]

Yet, in a different context, Stevenson was becoming actively involved with public issues during this period through his association with the Chicago Council on Foreign Relations. George Ball has described the Council as "an oasis of discontent in a complacent society brainwashed each morning [in the *Chicago Tribune*] by Colonel McCormick's insistent xenophobia." The Council on Foreign Relations exposed Stevenson to a variety of learned people, scholars, and men of affairs, all of whom tended toward the internationalist persuasion. Elected president of the Council in 1935, he regularly introduced guest speakers at its luncheon meetings, many of whom warned their listeners about the growing Fascist movement in Europe. By the end of the decade Stevenson was directly involved in the public debate over isolationism. It was the beginning of his preoccupation with what Carl McGowan has called "the great love" of Stevenson's life— international relations and foreign policy.[3]

Fervent moralism had already begun to characterize his speeches. In one address in 1938, Stevenson observed that if the Fascists should prevail, "then the future of the old world, and perhaps the new, is once more in the hands of the medieval warrior castes and the civilized era that began with the Renaissance is concluded." In October 1939, speaking in Bloomington a few weeks after the outbreak of the war in Europe, he declared that the fundamental issue was "whether freedom *can* be saved . . . whether the lights are doomed to go out one by one; and whether darkness is the destiny of man, as it has been before." In October 1940, as arguments raged over the question of extending American aid to beleaguered Britain, Stevenson bluntly told the Chicago League of Women Voters: "I think this is the most critical moment in our history. I think we are witnessing a death-struggle for control of the western world . . . between our traditions and pagan traditions never disciplined by the Roman Empire in the West or Christendom in the East." On another occasion he warned that Americans could not afford "to be indifferent to the triumph of a philosophy of life that denies the validity of every single principle we . . . hold dear. . . ." He predicted that the United States was "on the brink of a long ordeal, military, economic and spiritual, with mighty forces bent on world dominion. . . ."[4]

By 1940 Stevenson was working strenuously in the Chicago area for the Committee to Defend America by Aiding the Allies (the "William Allen White Committee"), which was engaged in a bitter propaganda battle with supporters of America First and the isolationist *Chicago Tribune.* Convinced that powerful elemental forces—good versus evil, order versus chaos—endlessly struggle throughout history for dominance, Stevenson viewed the war between Fascism and freedom in this context. Moreover his patriotism led him to argue that the United States had the responsibility to defend civilization against the latest barbarian assault. A few years later he interpreted the postwar international situation in similar terms, with Communism replacing Fascism as the enemy of freedom and order. In this respect, a certain moral absolutism characterized his thinking about foreign affairs. It was moderated, however, by a concurrent awareness of complexity, irony, and ambiguity which kept him from becoming an anti-Communist crusader of the Dulles variety. After the war he repeatedly emphasized that the world had become a vastly more complicated place, and he sometimes complained that the demands of politics forced him to oversimplify his views. "It is awfully difficult to say things that people can understand about foreign affairs—at least it is difficult for me," he confessed to Hamilton Fish Armstrong in 1953. "And my tendency is always to over-complicate, and then over-simplify, with the result that I am usually misunderstood in all directions."[5]

An absolutist, almost Calvinist strain coexisted in Stevenson's mind with sensitivity to the fact of diversity in the world, the role of chance in human affairs, and an abiding distrust of dogmatism.

Intuitively he sensed that fundamental conflicting forces have opposed one another at all times and in all places throughout history; intellectually he knew that the world was too complicated for its troubles to be described in such simplistic terms as good or evil. These conflicting perceptions—absolutism and relativism—plagued his thinking about international relations throughout his career. That is why he cannot be labeled as simply a "cold warrior."

World War II had a profound impact on Stevenson. First, he thought, it proved the importance of resisting aggression; second, it underscored the need to establish an effective international organization to keep the peace through collective security; third, it convinced him that another world conflict would destroy civilization itself. These conclusions shaped his approach to international relations after the war and imparted a sense of urgency to his thinking, for he knew that in the atomic age the stakes were high, the dangers acute. Certain that the failure of the democracies to oppose aggression in the thirties had made war inevitable, he was determined to do all he could to keep history from repeating itself. No war was "as tragic as that of 1939," he once remarked, "for, in retrospect, it seems almost a precise, sleep-walking repetition of the war of 1914." Thus, if "there is any realism . . . it must be to insure that such follies . . . such disasters never reoccur." Stevenson's wartime trips on government service left vivid memories of the consequences of appeasement. For example, he remembered Eschweiler, "a battered little town on the German frontier . . . Italy . . . wet, cold and bloody . . . the South Pacific . . . hot, steaming and bloody . . . the ghastly burns I had seen long before on those 'Pearl Harbor boys' in the rows of white beds in California." Recalling Woodrow Wilson's prophecy of another world war if the nations failed to organize to prevent it, he wondered, "Was this the everlasting destiny of man, indicted for his stupidity and sin, convicted, sentenced forever to kill or be killed?"[6]

Shortly after the war ended, Stevenson received an opportunity to help rekindle the Wilsonian dream. In September 1945 he traveled to London as deputy to former Secretary of State Edward R. Stettinius, Jr., part of the U.S. delegation to the Executive Committee of the United Nations Preparatory Commission, which was charged with drafting recommendations to implement the structure of the successor to Wilson's League of Nations. When Stettinius became ill and had to return home, Stevenson became the principal American delegate. He displayed patience, good humor, and resourcefulness in the negotiations, especially in dealing with the Soviet delegation. "I never saw a man handle the Russians like he did," one observer remarked. Chicago journalist Clifton Utley, who had earlier come to know Stevenson through the Council on Foreign Relations, was impressed by how Stevenson "changed his word choice, the structure of his argument" from one delegation to another, adding that it was "a virtuosity I had not noted before." "Although we had many disagreements and some bad hours with the Russians and a few of the other delegations, the area of agreement was very large," Stevenson reported to a friend in October. "I feel that on the evidence to date the Russians are entirely sincere about the United Nations, but it's a slow and tedious process to educate them in western ways and methods, and the negotiation becomes dreadfully trying at times."[7]

Stevenson continued his duties when the full Preparatory Commission convened in November. During these tedious weeks of hammering out a structure for postwar cooperation in the autumn chill of London, he took a cautiously optimistic view of the international situation. Speaking to an audience of British servicemen, he reminded them that "if ever there was a completely unnecessary war, a preventible war," it was the one that had just ended, and he emphasized that now the overriding question was whether the same mistakes would be made again. This speech revealed many of the major themes that would characterize Stevenson's thinking for the next twenty years: the new dangers and opportunities created by the war, the ominous technological revolution in means of destruction, the need for endless patience in international negotiations, and the potential significance of the United Nations.

> We must give time a chance to do its work. In history, there is no other healer. . . . The trouble is that there isn't as much time as there used to be . . . the age-old emotions of hatred, jealousy, suspicion and intolerance have at last been armed with weapons by which man can achieve his own complete destruction. . . . This is the point in human destiny to which all the glories and toils of the past have led us. . . . Man's mastery of science and the physical world has far outrun man's mastery of himself. . . .
>
> That is why it is the policy of the United States to get the UN organized and functioning as quickly as possible. . . . It will take the faith, confidence and energy of all of us to make it work. But it is the only practicable alternative. . . .

For peace is not merely the absence of war. It is not a static thing,
it is dynamic. It is something that has to be fought for all the time
. . . with high courage and fanatical patience.[8]

Stevenson knew that Soviet-American relations held the key to the
future. He deplored that mistrust of Russia was "becoming almost a
phobia" in some quarters. By 1950, however, he shared the general
opinion that the Soviet Union was intransigently hostile to the West
and that Communism posed as great a threat to freedom and peace as
Fascism. He told the British servicemen in 1945 that "we must make
progress in the difficult art of getting along" with the Russians,
because "the worst thing that could happen" would be for them to
"withdraw behind . . . walls of secrecy, to go it alone in isolation.
That's the road to disaster." But five years later (November 19, 1950)
he declared that the Soviet Union was "threatening political
thralldom through enslavement of men's minds, stalking democracy
throughout the world." What had happened in the interim to change
his mind about the Russians?[9]

2

In a word—plenty. Between 1945 and 1950 Soviet behavior caused
Stevenson to grow increasingly suspicious of the Kremlin's long-
range purposes. From a position of cautious optimism in 1945 concerning the possibilities for cooperation between Russia and the
West, he became convinced by 1950 that the USSR was bent on world
domination. Dean Acheson, President Truman's acerbic secretary of
state, wrote in his memoirs that the period 1941–1952 was "one of
great obscurity to those who lived through it." The "significance of
events," he emphasized, "was shrouded in ambiguity." Acheson was
seeking to justify the policies he helped to formulate by stressing the
uncertainties amid which decisions were made, but his observation is
important. International crises developed at a bewildering rate in the
late 1940s, and statesmen in the West tended to rely for guidance on
their recollections of the recent past, which demonstrated the futility
of efforts to appease aggressors. If in order to prevent a larger war it
was necessary to fight in Korea in 1950, Acheson and Truman were
ready. So was Stevenson. So were most American leaders. Such, they
believed, was the lesson they had learned from the tragic history of
their times. As early as 1943, Stevenson told the Chicago Council on

Foreign Relations: "Until there is collective force to police.the road to the better world, there must be individual force ready and determined to keep order until the [international] community is organized."[10]

Unlike some of his more militant contemporaries, Stevenson was a reluctant convert to the premises of the cold war. At least until sometime in 1948, or even 1949, he maintained that cooperation with the Soviet Union was possible, while admitting that it would be a long, frustrating process. In his 1943 speech to the Chicage Council, he said that he was comforted by "the fundamental fact" that Russia and the United States had a mutual interest in a peaceful postwar world. "Together we can do everything," he proclaimed. "Apart—well, it's unthinkable." He was still optimistic when he addressed the Chicago Bar Association in June 1945, after having dealt with Soviet diplomats at the San Francisco Conference on the United Nations. "It *is* difficult to work with the Russians," he readily acknowledged, and predicted that the Soviet Union "will attempt to surround her borders with friendly governments as a defense against the world of capitalism. . . ." But this prospect seemed less significant to Stevenson than the "earnestness" of the Soviet envoys at San Francisco, which he interpreted as a "measure of their sincerity and self-interest" in supporting the United Nations. The argument based on national self-interest was fundamental to his thinking. Writing from London in October 1945, he assured a Chicago labor leader that he was "convinced" that the Russians "mean business on the United Nations if for no other reason than that it serves their self-interest admirably, and I hope the failure of the peace conference will not occasion a waive [sic] of cynicism and isolationist sentiment in our country." In December 1945 Stevenson was interviewed in London by C. L. Sulzberger of the *New York Times*. Emphasizing his belief that "laws and institutions of international cooperation have to evolve out of . . . the common aspirations and experience of the peoples of the world," he told Sulzberger that the worst fate that could befall the UN would be for it "to become divided into two camps."[11]

Stevenson also frequently cited the traditional Russian suspicion of outsiders dating from Czarist times. Of course, the Soviet leaders intended to advance their aims, "many of them objectives of the Czars, to the utmost," he told the Chicago Council on Foreign Relations in March 1946. Still, he insisted, this proclivity was less important than the fact that they had "cooperated earnestly and energetically in building the United Nations." Moreover, he contended, the Russians, "like the United States, seem to trust us and want us to like and understand them. . . . They are realistic and respect power and prestige. They are victors and want spoils. And, most of all, they want a long period of recuperative peace." "I see no reason to be alarmed," he concluded. "There have always been competing ideologies. There is room for their system and ours to exist side by side." On another occasion he observed, "I think we are too impatient, too volatile. Making peace is harder than making war. . . . It will be secured only by the patient, slow development of mutual confidence and self-discipline for years to come." Late in 1946, he asserted: "As we look into 1947 there is no room for maudlin optimism. But we end the fateful year of 1946 in better heart than we entered it. Day by day . . . [the nations] are getting the habit of working together, getting to know each other better." By the end of 1947, however, he was less confident about the prospects for good relations.[12]

Speaking in Springfield, Illinois, in January 1947, Stevenson said he felt encouraged by two developments: the death of isolationism as a viable political force in the United States, and the steady growth of the United Nations. Turning to the subject of the Russians, he acknowledged their "aggressive, truculent and suspicious" behavior and noted they "expect severe economic disorder in this country and with it the extinction of capitalism." But he denied that conflict was inevitable, explaining: "If we can contain the dynamic, centrifugal force of Soviet power and the Soviet idea long enough it will slow down and evolve peacefully—and we can save the friendly Russian people and ourselves from catastrophe." There was "nothing to fear, save our own cupidity, short-sightedness and weakness, . . ." he emphasized. "There is nothing to fear but our own default." But when he spoke to the Investment Bankers Association that May, the international scene had darkened. President Truman, while asking Congress in March for massive aid for Greece and Turkey, depicted the Soviet Union as an implacable ideological foe of worldwide freedom. Stevenson defended the Greek-Turkish policy (the Truman Doctrine) in his speech to the bankers. He explained that the United States was prepared "through the 'Truman Doctrine' to intervene, unilaterally if necessary, at the request of the aggrieved, to support the principles of the United Nations charter." He still insisted, however, that Russia wanted peace "to bind up her awful wounds," and he continued to argue that mutual suspicions were to blame for the impasse in relations with Moscow. "I suppose the root of this hostile drift in American-Russian relations is fear," he said. "Our old fear and mistrust of Bolshevism is aggravated by Russia's stubborn, acquisitive behavior. Russia's old fear of capitalist encirclement and counterrevolution is aggravated by a suspicion that we would have been glad to see Russia and Germany both bleed to death in the war. . . . And so it goes . . . the vicious circle tightens. . . ."[13]

Ever since his days on the Chicago Council on Foreign Relations, Stevenson had been cultivating connections with the U.S. foreignpolicy establishment; his wartime government service and postwar work with the United Nations expanded his contacts. In those years he became acquainted with people like Dean Acheson, George Ball, Charles E. ("Chip") Bohlen, John Foster Dulles, Dorothy Fosdick, John J. McCloy, Archibald MacLeish, and numerous others. It was no coincidence that his address to the investment bankers in May contained ideas strikingly similar to those that George Kennan set forth in his article in the July 1947 issue of *Foreign Affairs*, "The Sources of Soviet Conduct." Echoing Kennan, Stevenson emphasized how "Communist ideology, ancient Russian habits of thought, and the internal conditions there, in combination, have produced a suspicion, fear, and a missionary zeal that underlie our difficulties with the Soviet Union." Stevenson agreed with Kennan that a major war was unlikely, but he thought it was imperative for the United States to formulate a policy of both resistance and assistance: "Resistance to further political expansion, because we know all too well that appeasement doesn't work . . . it will strengthen those who insist on further adventures, just as it strengthened Hitler." But he cautioned that "political resistance without economic assistance won't suffice . . . prosperity, like peace, is indivisible. . . . Because ours is the only nation that has the power to resist and the wealth to assist, the burden falls squarely on us."[14]

In June 1947 the United States announced the European Recovery Program (the Marshall Plan) to promote Europe's economic recovery and political stability. The Soviet Union declined to participate in the program or to allow any of its satellites to do so. In September, Stevenson was in New York for the meeting of the UN General Assembly. After one particularly exhausting session, he wrote despondently to Jane Dick, "I've just come into my dark and dreary rooms after a long post facto discussion of Vyshinsky's speech and delegation strategy. I'm weary, my eyes ache & I'm still smarting under that two hours of garbage Vysh. hurled at us this afternoon. All evening I've tried to act & talk calmly, coldly and not lose sight of the 'forest for the trees'—and now I want to burst loose with a torrent of profanity and abuse—No I don't. I want to go to bed and sleep." A few weeks later he told her, "Its a solemn year—this year of decision and I wish you were spending all your time and energy on the Marshall Plan—*so that someday we might have world government.*" In January he spoke at the Public Forum of the Chicago Athletic Club, vigorously defending the Marshall Plan as being in America's long-term best interest: "Because if we fail or refuse to make possible the return of Western Europe to self-support by obtaining a chief part of the goods she needs through the cooperation of our system of production and trade, it must turn in major part to the East . . . [and] the price of enforced dependence upon Eastern Europe would seem to mean for Western Europe, sooner or later, incorporation in the economic and political system of the Communists. It would mean a corresponding loss for the rest of the world." He remarked that a recent attack on the United States by the Soviet envoy during the recent General Assembly meeting was a defensive tactic: "Soviet dictators, like all dictators, want to keep their power and to increase it. To keep their own people in line, they must make it appear, therefore, that Soviet peace is constantly endangered. . . . Unless they can conjure up enemies, they cannot justify their power. . . . To combat disaffection and doubt, and maintain discipline in [the satellite states], their Russian-influenced governments needed this deluge of propaganda about the imperialist, warlike designs of the United States."[15]

It is difficult to say exactly how Stevenson assessed the course of international events in 1948 because he was preoccupied with politics in Illinois. The gubernatorial campaign forced him to concentrate on state issues and minimize references to foreign affairs. In a speech in Salem, Illinois, in July he said, "As one who struggled long and wearily in the post-war negotiations with the Russians, I thank God that President Truman has stood firm and taken a strong and positive position in the defense of the West against Soviet aggression." After the election he had even less time to talk about matters beyond the state's boundaries. One exception occurred in October 1949, when he addressed the Inland Daily Press Association in Chicago. By then a Communist *coup* had taken place in Czechoslovakia, the Russians had blocked land access to Berlin, and the long Chinese civil war was ending with the triumph of Mao's forces. Stevenson sought to assure his audience that the Soviet Union would not directly attack the West, but he acknowledged that "we *are* going to be incessantly engaged in an aggravating, exhausting cold war for longer than I like to contemplate." He said the cold war did have some positive effects: "It has caused the world to reexamine colonial policies and aspirations for freedom. It has drawn the Western community closer together. . . . It has kept the United States an alert and positive participant. It has even brought the dream of peace by world government closer to realization . . . [and] it has caused us in the midst of all the ferment of ideological conflict and realignment to look to our own housekeeping." Stevenson here anticipated a theme he would repeatedly stress in the 1950s: the critical importance of the underdeveloped nations. In February 1950 he told an audience at Kentucky's Centre College: "The preservation of the free world hangs upon our ability to win the allegiance of those millions . . . of people throughout the world who have not yet made their choice between our democratic system, on the one hand, and the promises which Communism offers, on the other." Their choice "will be mainly shaped by our own performance," he cautioned. "We won't resist the Soviet impact on the Western world with a schizophrenic society which protests its devotion to democratic ideals while it indulges in undemocratic practices, or which recoils in horror from an alien materialism but, blinded by its own material accomplishments, loses sight of its spiritual heritage."[16]

Stevenson's greatest concern in the period before the Korean War was whether the United States was prepared to resist aggression. The real question, he felt, was whether Americans realized that the world had irrevocably changed and that there could be no return to prewar habits of thought. Most of all, he worried about a revival of isolationist sentiment. To Stevenson the word "isolationism" stood for the whole syndrome of ignorance and appeasement that had led to war in 1939. In 1949 he published a long article on the subject in the *New York Times Magazine*, entitled "Challenge of a New Isolationism." Stevenson knew from personal experience in the Midwest how pervasive the isolationist element was in the American mind. In his article he deplored "a growing tendency to be internationally minded in principle but not in practice, to favor international cooperation in the abstract while opposing concrete steps to make it effective." While he termed the old isolationism "moribund," arguing that America had "come of age" since Pearl Harbor, he also thought that there was reason to fear "reincarnation of its spirit" in new guises. One danger signal was the "alarming identification of our policy with the containment of communism," which revealed an inadequate understanding by Americans of the complexity of the world. "Does public support for the foreign aid program represent genuine recognition of global economic problems," he asked, "or is it merely a reflection of the wide-spread fear of Communist Russia?" "Policy based on an anti-Russian crusade," he warned, "involves great dangers." What the American people must understand was that political demands for economy in government ignored the need for large-scale American spending programs to attack the root causes of war—hunger and poverty. "It is the tragedy of democratic countries that foreign policy is always, in time of peace, sacrificed to domestic policy," Stevenson noted. "Now my thesis is: There is no resurgence of blind, classical isolation in the Middle West, but there is a rapidly growing tax consciousness, and sooner or later we will have to face some stern issues. Can we, will we, pay the price of peace?" In one way or another, he continued to pose that question to his countrymen for the next sixteen years.[17]

3

The American people were asked to pay the ultimate price for peace in June 1950, when Communist North Korea invaded South Korea and the United States quickly entered the war under the United Nations banner. Stevenson supported President Truman's decision to intervene. "Stalin's offensive against the United States and the West would reach its crescendo in Korea," Secretary of State Acheson wrote in his memoirs, ". . . when, throwing off pretense, he made an attack in force through a satellite. . . ." Stevenson took an identical view of the crisis. Speaking at Vincennes, Indiana, in July he termed the North Korean attack "cynical unprovoked aggression." At the Illinois State Fair in August, he called for support of the war while criticizing those who blamed the country's ills on domestic traitors. "Partisanship is suffocating patriotism. . . . Tell the people that the enemy is without, not within, that we are outnumbered already, that the shadows are creeping over Asia, and that our problem is to fight Communism, not windmills. . . . Tell them that this is a battle for survival, not a witch hunt."[18]

The thirty-eighth parallel marked Stevenson's Rubicon in the cold war. He never completely freed his thinking from the shadow cast by the Korean War. More than anything else in the postwar period, it confirmed his belief that a firm response was the only remedy for "aggression." "We knew in 1950 that the communist attack on Korea was not an isolated event," he characteristically affirmed in one speech during the 1952 presidential campaign. "We knew it was part and parcel of a vast drive for world dominion that began long before . . . the North Koreans crossed the 38th parallel. It was intended that the Soviet-directed drive would carry right on through Korea in a few weeks—and far, far beyond, as the West sat indecisive and impotent." He drew the conventional analogy with the 1930s: "Why not? Wasn't that the history of the Japanese invasion of China; of Mussolini's invasion of Ethiopia; of Hitler's conquest in Europe?" In November 1951 he declared: "Adolph Hitler resurrected the malevolent doctrine of the master race. . . . And now comes imperial Communism, stalking freedom throughout the world." On another occasion he said he fully agreed with one of Truman's advisers who had remarked, "This attack on South Korea is like Hitler's reoccupation of the Rhineland."[19]

In the spring of 1952 Stevenson published an article called "Korea in Perspective" in *Foreign Affairs*. What would have happened, he asked, had the United States not intervened in Korea? The answer seemed obvious to him: "Our friends throughout Asia and in the Pacific would with perfect reason have doubted our intention to resist Soviet design elsewhere in that area, and they would of necessity have taken the path of appeasement. Disillusionment would also have swept Western Europe. . . . Then would not the Soviet Union, having challenged us successfully in Korea, have followed the challenge with another? . . . Munich would follow Munich. Our vacillation would have paralyzed our will and worked havoc in the community of like-minded nations." The overall objective of American foreign policy, Stevenson emphasized, must be to convince the Communist world that "other aggressions, disguised or direct, will meet the same response, and thus deter them from a perhaps fatal gamble." Appearing on the television program "Meet the Press" in March 1952, he made the same argument. Had the U.S. "not met this first armed challenge . . . [to] the principle of collective security," he commented, "appeasement" by other countries would have followed in its wake.[20]

His use of such charged words as "Munich" and "appeasement" suggests the powerful influence of the prewar era on Stevenson's view of the postwar world. As Dean Acheson pointed out, a pervasive ambiguity prevailed in this period. Statesmen, entrusted with the awesome responsibility of preventing another global conflict, tended to rely on the lessons of the past to justify their policies, for they were sure of at least one thing: failure to resist aggression had led to disaster in 1939. This certitude provided a convenient justification for the Truman Doctrine, the creation of the North Atlantic Treaty Organization, and the intervention in Korea. A habit of reasoning by analogy prevaded policy-making circles, often at the expense of original thinking. Communism was automatically likened to Fascism, Stalin to Hitler, in an irresistible process which was reinforced by the steady successsion of international crises around the globe between 1945 and 1950: Eastern Europe, Berlin, the Middle East, Greece, China. Then came Korea, the last link in the chain of events—a clear case of flagrant aggression. Now, so the reasoning in Washington went, was the time to meet force with force and thereby prevent the past from repeating itself. "If history has taught us anything," President Truman said, "it is that aggression anywhere in the world is a threat to peace everywhere in the world." There was bipartisan agreement on this basic point. A "far eastern Munich" in Korea would be fatal to the cause of freedom, warned conservative Republican Senator William Knowland. As time passed, this reasoning by analogy became a substitute for analysis of current international realities—with disastrous consequences for American foreign policy. In 1970 former President Lyndon Johnson still defended his administration's policy in Vietnam by making the old analogy with the 1930s: "Hitler's aggression almost destroyed the world, and we believe that Communist aggression will destroy it if someone doesn't stand up to it."[21]

Discussing the impact of Whig ideology on the minds of the leaders of the American Revolution, Bernard Bailyn has emphasized how these "beliefs, fears and perceptions became primary . . . in the sense of forming assumptions and expectations, of furnishing not merely the vocabulary but the grammar of thought, the apparatus by which the world was perceived." For the men of the Revolutionary era, Bailyn points out, the operative words which triggered their worst fears were "conspiracy" and "corruption." For the men of the cold war, the equivalent phrases were "Munich," "appeasement," and "aggression." In the 1950s, no less than in the 1760s, the perceptions that shaped political action originated from deep convictions rooted equally in history and imagination, in the bright light of reason and in the darkness of dreams punctuated by visions of catastrophe. In both eras this was "the apparatus by which the world was perceived."[22]

In recent years revisionist writers have furnished new perspectives on the origins of the cold war, providing refreshing contrasts to traditional anti-Communist interpretations. But what the revisionists generally fail to capture, H. Stuart Hughes has observed, is "something of the feel and taste of the late 1940s," when "hostility to Communism made sense in certain contexts . . . [given] the irrefutable realities of . . . Soviet domination of . . . East Central Europe." The statesmen of the early cold-war years had experienced the ordeal of total war. To equate Communism with Fascism, to see in Stalin another Hitler, was no doubt simplistic, perhaps utterly mistaken. But it was not unreasonable in a world still reeling from the convulsion of 1939–1945. So Adlai Stevenson might admit in 1952, "It's possible that we have made errors in Korea," but he would still insist, "I . . . say . . . that the question remains, could we have done anything else than we did on the 25th of June, 1950? My own opinion is that we did the only thing we dared to do at that time."[23]

The Korean intervention had a further significance in Stevenson's mind: it breathed life into the principle of collective security, thereby signaling to the world that the UN would not go the way of the League of Nations. By sending troops to Korea, the United Nations had "passed the supreme test which confronts any organization devised for collective security," Stevenson asserted in October 1950. "When the chips were down . . . it acted." He glossed over the fact that the UN Army was essentially an American and South Korean force, commanded by an American, General Douglas MacArthur, who took his orders from Washington, not the United Nations. Stevenson could rationalize these matters because he realized that the effectiveness of the UN depended on America's willingness to support it; therefore, he could argue that the Korean crisis did mark a turning point in the young life of the organization, despite the failure of most of its members to make more than a token contribution to the forces in Korea. Several interrelated considerations thus justified the Korean War in Stevenson's eyes: the need to give credibility to the idea of collective security, the need to demonstrate that the United Nations was not another impotent international Alliance unsupported by force, and the need to demonstrate that the United States had learned its lesson and henceforth would not shirk its international responsibilities.[24]

Then politics entered the picture. With President Truman himself urging him to seek the Democratic nomination in 1952, Stevenson was in a dilemma. He wanted another term as governor of Illinois, but he was afraid that a Republican administration would fail to resist the siren song of isolationism. Carl McGowan has said that Stevenson felt somewhat uncomfortable running against Dwight Eisenhower in 1952 because, initially at least, he felt that he and Eisenhower agreed on the essentials of foreign policy. In the months prior to the national political conventions, however, it was by no means clear that Eisenhower would be the GOP nominee. Stevenson feared that the Republican candidate would be Senator Taft, whom he identified—perhaps unfairly—with the discredited forces of isolationism. The "threat of Taft is occasion for anxiety for us all," he remarked to one correspondent in June 1952. He confided to Jane Dick, "I'm saying nothing more about my availability so that I can get out if its Ike and go if its Taft. . . . I'm praying it will be Ike even tho he's been an awful disappointment so far. . . . But as Pres. I'm sure he would not junk the foreign policy. . . ." The prospect of facing Eisenhower in the general election relieved Stevenson's fear about a resurgence of isolationism, but it also deprived him of the clear-cut debate on foreign policy he expected in a contest with Taft.[25]

The triumph of the "internationalist wing" of the GOP in 1952 put Stevenson in a difficult situation. He soon discovered a host of specific issues on which to criticize Eisenhower. Indeed, by the time of the 1956 election he was convinced that the administration was utterly inept in its conduct of foreign relations. But he could never overcome the fact that he and Eisenhower, for all their differences in emphasis, agreed on the essential ingredients of foreign policy—a strong American presence in the world, cooperation with the United Nations, unyielding opposition to Communist "aggression." As a result, Stevenson was condemned to a "me too, but . . ." position which not only caused him enormous political frustration but also reduced the possibilities for a true dialogue with the Eisenhower administration on American foreign policy in the 1950s.

4

During the 1952 presidential contest the Republicans repeatedly promised dramatic changes in American foreign policy if they were returned to office. Their principal spokesman on foreign affairs, John

Foster Dulles, asserted that the goal of the United States should be to defeat Communism, not just to contain it. But Dulles did not specify how victory would be achieved; instead he relied on such vague statements as "we should let truths work in and through us. We should be dynamic, we should use ideas as weapons. . . ." Whether such rhetoric had much to do with the Republican triumph is doubtful. A better guess is that the electorate turned to Eisenhower in the hope that he could find a way to end the Korean War. Late in the campaign Ike announced that he would go to Korea if elected, and this pledge apparently had a great impact on the voters. A truce was negotiated in Korea a few months after Eisenhower took office, but the main lines of United States foreign policy remained unchanged under the new administration. Secretary of State Dulles spoke of "liberating" Eastern Europe from Communism, threatened "massive retaliation" against the Soviet Union, promised a "new look" in the defense establishment, and asserted that this country was prepared to go "to the brink" of war. But what did all this rhetoric mean?[26]

Stevenson quickly concluded it meant very little. He charged the Republicans with substituting tough talk for action and accused them of being more interested in reducing the budget than anything else. "If it is really true that we have embarked on a new policy, and I am by no means sure from the budget figures, I think it demands more and more public scrutiny," he wrote in January 1954 to George Kennan (the original theorist of containment). "At least we should know what it really is, economic or defense. Meanwhile, I suppose our Allies are guessing, and very nervously." Late in 1955, he accurately predicted that future historians, while noting "sharp changes in tone and manner" of Republican foreign policy, would recognize its essential continuity with the containment policy of the Truman administration.[27]

Stevenson found Dulles's rhetoric an irresistible target for criticism and quips. "What if we had relied exclusively on a policy of 'massive retaliation' since the close of World War II?" he asked at a Democratic conference in March 1954. "Would we have resorted to global atomic war in order to meet the Communist threat in Greece and Turkey? To counter the Berlin blockade? To resist aggression in Korea? If the answer is no, then the so-called 'new look' in foreign policy is no 'new look' at all, but merely a continuation of the policy of adapting our methods of resistance to the method of attack. . . ." "It may be that they don't mean what they say," he added. "But issues of life and death should be clarified and not clouded . . . security in our age cannot be brought by slogans and gimmicks." Speaking on national radio and television in Apriil 1955 during the Quemoy-Matsu crisis, Stevenson noted there had been "plenty of massive verbal retaliation," which had "alarmed our friends [in Europe] a good deal more than it has deterred the aggressors." He also deplored the jingoism of the Republicans' rhetoric, warning that as long as "we over-militarize our international thought and statement, for so long will our efforts prove futile and our motives suspect." He maintained that President Truman's Point Four program of economic assistance was "an idea far more stirring, far more powerful, than all the empty slogans about liberation and retaliation and unleashing [Chiang Kai-shek on the Chinese mainland] rolled together."[28]

Despite his scathing indictments of the Eisenhower administration, Stevenson shared many of the basic premises of his Republican opponents. Frustrated by his failure to attract more public attention to his critique of the Eisenhower-Dulles policies, Stevenson asked his old friend Archibald MacLeish for advice in August 1955: "Granted that it is ends rather than means that we should be talking about today—and that the great common end is peace—how does one build a campaign on this?" Stevenson blamed his troubles on the "one-party press," and lamented the difficulty of trying to talk in depth about complicated issues during a campaign. His complaints were valid, to be sure; but they were not the only reasons for his plight. The administration constantly declared it wanted "peace"—so did he. Who did not want peace? The administration saw Communism as the main obstacle to achieving peace—so did he. It favored cooperating with the United Nations in the search for peace while reserving the right to act independently when necessary—so did he. Thus, although Stevenson could endlessly assail Eisenhower's conduct of foreign affairs, the political impact of his criticism was minimal. He was restricted to challenging the means—not the ends or basic assumptions—of foreign policy, and most voters apparently saw it as mere quibbling on his part when he did so. They certainly did not see it as a sufficient reason to turn the Republicans out of the White House.[29]

Stevenson's anti-Communist views were both modified and reinforced in 1953 when he took an extensive trip through Asia, the Middle East, and Europe. "It seems to me that it's terribly important for anyone who is speaking or writing about contemporary affairs to understand something of . . . this revolution that's going on in the colonial areas of the world, and in Asia particularly," he explained to newsman Edward P. Morgan early in 1953. So he embarked on a well-publicized safari of self-education, which also had the advantage of keeping his name before the public. He was bewildered by all that he had experienced during his travels. "How does one express coherent, orderly, confident views about this vast, tortured, teeming, frightened segment of our world," he asked T. S. Matthews of *Time* magazine in a letter written from Hong Kong. Stevenson had to confront the reality of Communism's appeal to the awakening colonial peoples. He came back from his travels with a vastly heightened sense of the importance of the underdeveloped regions which colored all his subsequent thinking about foreign affairs. In a nationally broadcast report on his trip after he returned home, he cautioned Americans that the "ideological conflict in the world doesn't mean much to the masses. Anti-Communist preaching wins few hearts. . . ." He noted that people in countries like India, Indonesia, and Burma "don't accept the thesis that everyone has to choose sides. . . . Nor do I believe that we should press alliances on unwilling allies." Yet, in his Godkin lectures at Harvard a few months later, he referred to India's "unrealistic but persistent neutralism," as if it were somehow immoral. And in a position paper issued under his name during the 1956 campaign, he concluded a critique of Eisenhower's policy toward the new nations by saying, "[The Administration] has expended its energies in brittle military pacts and self-righteous preachments—while Communism and neutralism have spread." Once more Stevenson was reduced to criticizing the means of foreign policy, rather than the basic assumptions behind it. He clearly saw the futility of "brittle military pacts and self-righteous preachments" in seeking friends in the third world, but neither could he accept the legitimacy of neutralism in the cold war.[30]

Stevenson wanted to focus his 1956 presidential campaign on Eisenhower's conduct of foreign affairs, but his political advisers disagreed. They urged him to minimize foreign affairs in his speeches and concentrate on the President's domestic record. Stevenson admitted to his confidants that he was dubious about this strategy: "I am convinced that the administration is most vulnerable in that area [foreign policy] and that it is also the most important area," he told J. William Fulbright in June 1956. "We ought to be able to devise some means of exploiting it for political advantage, national benefit and voter education." But Stevenson never found an effective "means of exploiting" the administration's record because—for all his misgivings about it—he was hard pressed to offer the electorate a specific, substantial alternative to those policies. His dilemma was most apparent when war broke out in the Middle East during the final days of the 1956 campaign.[31]

The situation in the Middle East had steadily deteriorated since the United States withdrew its offer to help Egypt build a high dam on the Nile River at Aswan. Presumably, this decision was prompted by anger in Washington over Egyptian President Gamal Abdel Nasser's flirtations with the Communist bloc. Nasser responded on July 26, 1956, by nationalizing the Suez Canal, explaining that Egypt needed the revenue from the canal to finance the Aswan project. Stevenson was deeply concerned about these developments, but—uncertain of their political utility and fearful of disrupting diplomatic efforts to resolve the situation—he did not discuss the issue in the campaign. At a press conference on September 17, he remarked, "I do not think that any comment by me at this crucial moment would serve a constructive purpose." Privately he was angry and alarmed. "The deterioration of our relations [with Western Europe] over Suez is frightening," he confided to Philip Noel-Baker, a British friend, on Ocotber 13. "I have been in a quandary as to how to handle foreign affairs during this campaign and I am both ill informed and reluctant to cause [the Eisenhower administration] any embarrassment. . . . As you can imagine, my esteem for Mr. Dulles has not increased, and I am tempted to do an analytical attack on the whole conduct of our relations with the Middle East which culminated so disastrously."[32]

Encouraged by a letter he received in mid-October from Dean Acheson, urging him to shift the target of his faltering campaign to the area of foreign affairs, Stevenson finally began to talk about the Middle East. In a hard-hitting speech at Cincinnati on Ocotber 29, he said, "We live in a watershed in history—and no mans knows in what direction the elemental forces that are loose in the world will turn. This much is plain: The West, so long the dominant force in world affairs, has gone on the defensive. . . . At the same time the Communist sphere has been growing. . . ." He charged Eisenhower with concealing the gravity of the Middle East crisis: "Why didn't the President tell us the truth? Why hasn't he told us frankly that what has happened in these past few months is that the Communist rulers of Soviet Russia have accomplished a Russian ambition that the czars could never accomplish? Russian power and influence have moved into the Middle East—the oil tank of Europe and Asia and the great bridge between East and West. . . . Instead of fresh ideas and creative thinking about the great struggle of our century, our approach to world affairs has remained sterile and timid. . . ."[33]

But what fresh ideas or creative thinking did Stevenson contribute to the discussion of the Middle East at this crucial juncture? Even allowing for the disadvantages he faced as challenger to an incumbent President, Stevenson failed to provide an alternative to the Republican's Middle East policies. Instead he only lamented Russian gains in the region and implied that Eisenhower was to blame for everything that had happened there. This was intellectually inadequate and politically ineffective. Meanwhile, after weeks of inconclusive negotiations attempting to resolve the impasse over Suez, Israel launched on October 29 a so-called preventive strike against Egypt. Britain and France, fearful of seeing their oil pipeline shut off, sent in troops to seize the canal. The Russians hinted that they might intervene on the side of Egypt. Suddenly America was embroiled in a full-blown crisis on the eve of the presidential election.[34]

The disastrous developments in the Middle East invited vigorous public debate over the administration's foreign policies, but Stevenson was unable to capitalize on the opportunity. Indeed he found himself in a political "no win" position. If he strongly assailed Eisenhower's diplomacy, the Republicans—and much of the general public—would charge him with playing politics during a national crisis. If he supported the administration, he would appear to be in fundamental agreement with it, and most people would see no reason to vote for him. Stevenson—who was trailing Eisenhower in the polls anyway—chose to go on the offensive. In a nationally broadcast speech on November 1, he maintained that the fighting in Egypt demonstrated "the bankruptcy of our policy," gave the Soviet Union a great diplomatic triumph, and threatened to undermine the Western alliance. He contended that a more farsighted policy might have averted hostilities. But the speech lost whatever political impact it might have had when Stevenson concluded with the ambiguous assertion: "I say that we now have an opportunity to use our great potential moral authority, our own statesmanship, the weight of our economic power, to bring about solutions to the whole range of complex problems . . . in the Middle East." Was rhetorical reliance on "moral authority" likely to win votes away from an administration which defended its policies with similar moralistic rhetoric? A study of the 1956 election conducted by the Brookings Institution concluded that Stevenson's allusion to "moral authority" cost him any slim chance he had of winning, because he seemed unable to offer the electorate an alternative to Eisenhower's policy "at the critical time of choice."[35]

After the election Stevenson cited numerous reasons for his defeat: the exhausting battle with Senator Estes Kefauver in the primaries; his advisers' insistence that there were no votes in foreign affairs; the partisan press; the Republicans' skillful use of public relations techniques. "I really don't believe Eisenhower would have been too hard to beat if he had been chopped up a little beforehand," Stevenson ruefully remarked to Senator John Sparkman (his 1952 running mate). "Our curves were in the right direction until the stampede started for refuge with Eisenhower—from Eisenhower's mistakes." He admitted to Dean Acheson that it had been "a mistake" to refrain from talking about foreign affairs until late in the campaign, "but it appeared from most of our advice that the people were content with 'peace' and not interested in details."[36]

Was the problem only one of "details"? What prevented Stevenson from questioning the essentials of Republican foreign policy—i.e., its moralism and fervent anti-Communism? Since he recognized that the administration was unnecessarily rigid and self-righteous in its conduct of foreign relations, he might have gone on to question the whole moralistic approach to foreign policy. But such a critique was beyond his capability. For Stevenson himself was firmly grounded in the moralistic tradition, tied to a Wilsonian view of America and the world, and thus limited in his ability to criticize the underlying premises of the Eisenhower administration. All too often he was reduced to attacking its flanks, rather than the main body of its controlling assumptions. The American people deserved, and the times demanded, more.

5

Shortly after his defeat in 1956 Stevenson confided to Agnes Meyer that he was "unhappy with the fact that so little has been written or said about my continuing ideological value and political usefulness to the party." Unless "the rank and file find expression somehow," he predicted, "neither I nor my expressed views will have any further value. . . ." The course of foreign affairs during Eisenhower's second term reinforced Stevenson's anxieties. He feared that the combination of the public's disinterest and the administration's ineptitude might cause the United States to lose the cold war without a shot being fired. But his only solution was to return the Democrats to power. "Personally I strongly feel that a sustained and vigorous scrutiny and criticism of the administration, not only in Congress but throughout the country, will be necessary if we cherish any hopes of winning in 1960," he emphasized to a Democratic congressman early in 1957.[37]

His fear of losing influence within the party, coupled with concern over the direction of public policy, encouraged Stevenson to lend his support to the creation of the Democratic Advisory Council in 1957. Besides Stevenson, the membership included former President Truman, Averell Harriman, Herbert Lehman, G. Mennen Williams, and—in a special "consultant" role—Eleanor Roosevelt. They all believed that the Democratic congressional leaders, Sam Rayburn and Lyndon Johnson of Texas, were insufficiently critical of the Eisenhower administration's policies. Stevenson saw the DAC as a means of keeping his own views in circulation, both within the party and among the public. Thomas Finletter, one of his reliable "brain trusters," told Stevenson that the DAC could become "the machine which will carry on a great part of the 1960 campaign." But the DAC failed to fulfill its members' expectations. In practice, one historian concludes, it proved to be "virtually an institutionalized version of the old 'Finletter group' "—i.e., those loosely associated individuals drawn from the ranks of government, the legal profession, and the universities who had drafted public policy for the Democrats for a number of years. Moreover, while Stevenson's thinking on international affairs remained solidly anti-Communist, it was beginning to differ in important ways from that of Democratic hard-liners, like Dean Acheson and Paul Nitze, who stressed armaments and military strength. As DAC foreign-policy statements began to reflect their views more than his own, he lost interest in the organization. He was learning that, as he had feared, a twice-beaten candidate had little real influence on party policy.[38]

In November 1957 the Eisenhower administration invited Stevenson to join its preparations for a forthcoming conference in Paris of NATO heads of state. The Western alliance was in trouble, in large part because of the Suez fiasco. There was also disagreement among the alliance partners over nuclear strategy and weapons' disposition.

Stevenson interpreted the administration's invitation, couched in terms of bipartisanship, as a political ploy designed to embarrass him, but he felt he had to accept. "To refuse . . . would have been bad citizenship and therefore maybe bad politics," he remarked to his friend Barry Bingham of the *Louisville Courier-Journal.* "But it is a melancholy job surrounded by people who mean me no good." And he lamented to Arthur Schlesinger, Jr., "I wish I *had* the *idea* which is so desperately needed to give NATO a new heart and confidence—and perhaps, most importantly, others a new loyalty and confidence in the West." It was almost an acknowledgment of his inability to distinguish his position in foreign affairs from that of the Republicans whom he regarded with contempt.[39]

Stevenson kept a diary during the short time he spent in Washington in late 1957 planning for the NATO conference. After one working session he wrote, "The atmosphere in the room . . . was more one of concern with how we made a profession of good will and confidence than the reality. But I was pleased to note audible declarations that the meeting had to have more than a military content." It was his opposition to what he termed an "over-militarized" foreign policy which separated Stevenson from both the Eisenhower administration and the Acheson-Nitze element in his own party. "I am troubled by the lack of a sense of urgency," he informed Dulles. Contrasting the present situation with the political climate he had encountered in Washington in 1933 and 1941, he observed, "Both times the atmosphere was different. I wish it was now. The response to Sputnik, etc. doesn't seem to meet the measure of the emergency. It seems to be compounded largely of more missiles and more reassurances." He outlined his principal disagreements with the administration: overreliance on military alliances and nuclear weapons; underreliance on the economic dimension of foreign policy, especially with regard to Asia, Africa, and Latin America; the imperative need for greater efforts to achieve arms control. On December 5 Stevenson told Dulles, "I hope very much that at NATO the U.S. can express something more than 'interest' in the less-developed, uncommitted areas where the cold war is hot." The next day he urged him to encourage the President to "loudly declare that he thinks NATO has a larger purpose than defense; that its purpose is peace and progress . . . that in this shrinking world . . . the rich must help the poor; and that this is a higher, better goal for NATO than the accumulation of nuclear weapons, however necessary." By acknowledging that nuclear weapons were "necessary," Stevenson undermined whatever impact his observations might have had on the administration's thinking. He sensed that its priorities were wrong, but not wholly wrong. That was his perennial dilemma.[40]

Stevenson was invited to accompany the U.S. delegation to Paris. He decided not to make the trip, probably agreeing with Thomas Finletter's opinion that it would be a waste of time. "My guess is that the admin. will not take any of these suggestions of yours, in which case you will have done everything you can," Finletter pointed out, while advising Stevenson to go to Paris only "if you believe that they really mean to carry through with what they say they do." Finletter's skepticism was well grounded. A telephone conversation between the President and Secretary of State Dulles during this period bluntly reveals the administration's view of Stevenson. Paraphrasing part of Stevenson's public statement concerning his role in planning for the NATO conference, Eisenhower asked Dulles, "What the hell does that mean? I think the man is fuzzy."[41]

Eisenhower was not alone in regarding Stevenson as somehow fuzzy in his thinking. Many of the self-styled "realists" in both parties had a similar opinion of him. This perception was widespread among the intimates of John F. Kennedy, and Stevenson knew it. After Kennedy was nominated for President in 1960, Stevenson sought to persuade him of the soundness of his views. For he wanted nothing as much as an opportunity to shape foreign policy—preferably as secretary of state—in a new Democratic administration. But first, he had to bring his ideas to Kennedy's attention.

George Ball suggested how this might be done. He recommended that a detailed foreign-policy document reflecting Stevenson's views and bearing his name be prepared for Kennedy prior to the election. Ball knew that Stevenson wanted the State Department job. Emphasizing that the G.O.P. ticket of Nixon and Henry Cabot Lodge would undoubtedly claim special expertise in foreign affairs, Ball told Stevenson that "your bargaining position [with Kennedy] will probably never be higher than it is at the moment." Stevenson enthusiastically agreed with this strategy of "sponsoring" a foreign-affairs position book. He even implied to at least one friend that the idea had been his own. "Very confidentially," he informed Barbara Ward in August 1960, "Kennedy has . . . eagerly accepted my suggestion that some study be commenced of the problems that he will face and the steps he must take . . . to lay hands on our foreign policy."[42]

The document that emerged was entitled "Components of a New

Foreign Policy." It was an extensive summary of the international situation on all fronts and contained specific recommendations for future policy. Its main theme was that of a "world in revolution," due to the emergence of "two-thirds of the world's peoples . . . from centuries of domination by a handful of power centers." Given this reality, the overriding task facing U.S. policy makers was whether the nations of the third world would "choose true independence or lapse into a darker colonialism directed from Moscow or Peiping in the hope of more rapid economic development." A second, closely related question was, How could the U.S. gain the confidence of these peoples without appearing to "impose our own political or economic ideas" upon them? The document also insisted that foreign policy must rest upon a better understanding with our European allies: "Unless we can insure that the Western powers will join with us in a common effort to achieve arms control and disarmament, hope for a lasting peace will grow dimmer and dimmer."[43]

Stevenson did not personally write "Components of a New Foreign Policy," but it accurately reflected his thinking. Through this means, he was trying to bring to Kennedy's attention the ideas that he had hoped to publicize under the auspices of the Democratic Advisory Council. By 1960 the consensus that had been attained in the early fifties on foreign policy was breaking down. Although the cold war still colored Stevenson's thinking, his views were increasingly at variance with those of the hard-line cold warriors. A silent struggle was now underway for Kennedy's favor between the so-called soft- and tough-minded foreign-policy strategists. "Components of a New Foreign Policy" was intended to legitimize the ideas of those persons who questioned the reliance on military force—or the threat of such force—in virtually every crisis. The other purpose of the document, of course, was to enhance Stevenson's stature in Kennedy's eyes and thereby enhance his chances of becoming secretary of state. By attempting to nudge the Democratic nominee in the direction of reducing tensions with the Soviets, in stressing goods and grain rather than guns, Stevenson was groping for a way out of the sterile conceptions that had frozen American foreign-policy formulation for more than a decade. To gain additional credit with Kennedy, he hit the campaign trail hard in the fall, delivering numerous speeches for the Democratic ticket. "My own efforts have been unqualified," he told Barbara Ward late in the campaign, "and I assume will not be overlooked or underestimated in the Kennedy camp."[44]

Unfortunately for Stevenson's hopes, all his efforts failed to gain him the State Department job. According to Theodore Sorensen, Stevenson's refusal to endorse Kennedy prior to the Democratic convention killed any chance he might have had to gain the position. After the election, the prize that Kennedy offered him was the ambassadorship to the United Nations. At the UN, Stevenson's international prestige would be valuable to the administration, and the assignment in New York would keep him out of the Washington spotlight as well. Presumably Kennedy felt that he could afford a "soft" thinker on the Hudson, but not on the banks of the Potomac.[45]

Stevenson did not want to take the United Nations position. He explained his reservations about it in a letter to a friend before the election, insisting that he did not "deprecate the organization or its importance," but adding "I simply don't want to work there myself. Perhaps it is because I don't like to carry other people's briefs anymore." For he realized perfectly well that the UN ambassadorship was, as George Ball put it, "largely ritualistic and ministerial" in nature, no matter what assurances Kennedy might give to the contrary. But Stevenson also knew, as Ball had warned him in July, that to decline the position would be construed "as sour grapes on your part." Somehow he had to convince Kennedy to make the job more substantive, so that if he took it he could count on being more than a mouthpiece for the administration.[46]

Stevenson's notes on a talk with the President-elect, dated December 8, 1960, reveal his state of mind: "I'll be frank—Expected Sec. State—Something of value to you and country. . . . Most difficult assignment—99 nations—in trouble everywhere. . . . All problems affect UN—[policy] made *here*—stuck there." On December 10, he told Kennedy by telephone that the first precondition for his acceptance of the post would be for the administration to recognize the UN "as center of our foreign policy." Following another telephone conversation with Kennedy and Secretary of State-designate Dean Rusk on December 11, he noted, "My tastes & experience—executive, administrative & creative—not legislative or representational." But he indicated that he was "willing to try if JK & Sec. want me to—*and* are sympathetic to following suggestions." He then made ten recommendations for bolstering the position, including cabinet rank, an option to attend meetings of the National Security Council, and a "free hand" in staff selection. In all these ways he hoped to elevate the UN ambassadorship to the "main stream of policy making." And once more he stressed the need to "preserve UN as center of our foreign policy ag[ainst] Soviet attacks," rather than employing it "not just occasionally in desperation as Dulles did." Finally, on December 12, Stevenson's appointment was publicly announced. William McCormick Blair, Jr., his longtime friend and administrative assistant, recalls that Stevenson remarked to him, "I told you I'd never take that UN job!" Both men just laughed.[47]

Why did he accept it? Because he was an activist, a political wheelhorse, who preferred to toil on the periphery of public affairs than retire to the sidelines. Perhaps he convinced himself that he would indeed be given opportunities to help make policy as a new administration led the country into a new decade. Last but not least, Stevenson knew that Kennedy needed him on his team—or more accurately, needed the support of the "Stevenson wing" of the party. For all these reasons, in January 1961 he took up residence in the living quarters of the U.S. Permanent Representative to the United Nations, despite his reluctance "to carry other people's briefs anymore."

6

The recurring theme in many of the public addresses that Stevenson delivered between 1961 and 1965 was the dream of creating an international community. "If there can be said to be a wave of the future for mankind," he told the International Astronomical Union in 1961, "I believe it is in [the] principle of community." He insisted that the nations of the world must overcome their "jungle habits of the past," and learn to "join their sovereign wills . . . in common obedience to the community's rules." In the age of superpowers and superbombs, Stevenson warned, the only alternative to cooperation was catastrophe. Speaking at Boston University's commencement ceremonies in June 1962, he asserted, "What I believe we are striving toward, however haltingly, is something much more intricate and much more tolerant than empire, but less dangerous and less highly charged than this present state of cold war. Perhaps the best word for it is *community*." While acknowledging that this goal would require "an infinity of patient diplomacy on both sides," he maintained that the eventual outcome would more than justify the labor to achieve it—"a new international order in which the old empires are replaced not by still another wave of empires, but by a community of the equal and the free and the tolerant."[48]

Stevenson encountered rough seas en route to the ideal of international community during his tenure at the UN. The story of his frustrations has been told in detail elsewhere, but a few observations may here be in order. The fundamental point to remember is that Stevenson was an official spokesman for the United States government, an advocate of and apologist for its foreign policies. He took his role seriously and was scrupulously loyal to the Presidents under whom he served. Although he sometimes complained to intimates about the frustrations of his position, grumbling was part of his character; he had always been something of a complainer as his friends all knew. Nevertheless, he was genuinely disappointed over the failure of the White House to consult him on policy matters. He felt he was being underutilized.[49]

Almost from the outset a few people urged him to quit. "Your great value to the country has always been that of an idea man, and in an ambassadorial post that value is necessarily lost," Gerald Johnson pointed out to him in December 1961. "So get the hell out and into some place where you will be a voice and not merely an echo." If Stevenson wished to leave, he had several opportunities. Late in 1961 he considered resigning in order to run in 1962 for the Illinois seat in the U.S. Senate. Earlier in the year he has been humiliated when he denied in the Security Council that the United States had been directly involved in the abortive attempt to invade Cuba and overthrow Fidel Castro. According to Jane Dick, after his speech a shaken Stevenson said to her, "You heard my speech today? Well, I did not tell the whole truth; I did not know the whole truth. . . . Now, my credibility has been compromised, and therefore my usefulness. Yet how can I resign at this moment and make things still worse for the President?" A few weeks later he admitted to the sociologist David Riesman, "I have had my troubles, and begin to wonder how long it takes to 'season' some of the young liberals." After deciding against the Senate venture, he remarked to William Blair, "I must say I was a little tempted to be my own boss again, but the President was very good about it and may make my life a little easier than it is at present." His relations with President Kennedy, however, continued to be strained. When Senator Hubert Humphrey suggested that he try to arrange more personal meetings with the President, Stevenson replied, "Maybe I will do it, but it doesn't come easily. Not that I don't enjoy it, but I feel that if he wants my point of view he will ask for it." The comment reveals a great deal about Stevenson's attitude toward Kennedy, as does his terse remark after a meeting with the President, "That young man, he never says 'please' and he never says 'I'm sorry!' "[50]

Another opportunity for Stevenson to resign his post—but not under circumstances of his own choosing—came in December 1962, when the journalists Stewart Alsop and Charles Bartlett published an account of the secret top-level executive conferences that had taken place during the recent Cuban missile episode. The article quoted an unnamed source as saying, "Adlai wanted a Munich," in reference to Stevenson's suggestion that one way to relieve the situation might be for the United States to consider dismantling its missiles in Turkey if the Soviets agreed to remove theirs from Cuba. President Kennedy—who was acquainted with Bartlett—may have authorized this leak in order to force Stevenson out of the administration. If so, the President's strategy backfired. "What the article doesn't say," Stevenson protested on a television program, "is that I opposed . . . an invasion of Cuba at the risk of nuclear war until the peace-keeping machinery of the UN had been used." Kennedy, perhaps in response to advice he received from Arthur Schlesinger, Jr., who remained a friend of both men, wrote Stevenson on December 5 to tell him that his "continued work at the United Nations will be of inestimable value" to the country and assured him of "my fullest confidence." The letter was released to the press. Stevenson had won a tactical victory of sorts over those persons in the administration who saw him as fuzzy or soft on issues of foreign policy. On December 8 he informed Barbara Ward that "my friends" had "quickly converted a hatchet into a boomerang," and added that he felt that "there is little left for me to worry about as far as my position in the United Nations is concerned, or at the White House for that matter."[51]

Stevenson told Ralph McGill of the *Atlanta Constitution* that the Cuban crisis demonstrated the value of the United Nations, "because it is only through the UN that the exposure of the missiles could be dramatized, and made indeed visible to all of the Afro-Asians, whom the Soviet Union had spent so much money and time neutralizing." Such consolations helped him persevere. In the opinion of George Ball, however, the Cuban affair had a lasting effect: "After the Cuban missile crisis Adlai was only going through the motions. His role had become ritualistic. From then on he knew he was not going to have an impact on foreign policy—which was what was most important to him. Washington was a force of its own and he was not part of it."[52]

After Kennedy's assassination had elevated Lyndon Johnson to the presidency, Stevenson thought that he would enjoy an improved relationship with the White House, both personally and in policy matters. "Stevenson said to me that he thought he would play a much larger role in foreign policy than he had been permitted to play under Kennedy," Arthur Schlesinger, Jr. has recalled. "I think he felt that his own generation was coming back to power, and that those bright, hard, definite young men who made him vaguely uneasy would fade out of the picture." Harlan Cleveland, who as assistant secretary of state for International Organization Affairs, was then serving in a liaison capacity between the State Department and the U.S. mission at the UN, remembers Stevenson remarking, "Lyndon Johnson, we're both politicians, we're of the same generation, he knows what makes me tick and I know what makes him tick. We can get along."[53]

Gradually, however, it became apparent to Stevenson that his influence on policy making was not increasing; if anything, it decreased as time passed. President Johnson shared his predecessor's perception of the role of the United Nations. Like Kennedy, Johnson saw the UN as a valuable forum for articulating and justifying American foreign policy, but not as a major resource in formulating it. Consequently Stevenson was condemned to the role of advocate. He had to rely on middle men to communicate his thoughts to the White House. "I am presuming to send you a copy of a telegram I sent to Ellsworth Bunker on the Dominican Republic," he informed presidential aide Bill Moyers in June 1965. "I have an impression that my views seldom come to the President's attention." Thus had the high hopes of late 1963 been dashed by 1965.[54]

Cuba, the Congo, Cyprus, the Middle East, the Article 19 controversy over member states' peace-keeping assessments, the Dominican Republic—Stevenson was confronted by one crisis after another during his tenure at the UN. Vietnam was only one of many problems competing for his attention; in late 1964 and early 1965, it had not yet become the dominant issue in American politics. But Stevenson was increasingly preoccupied with it in the last months of his life. The Vietnam question illustrates the difficulties inherent in his position as spokesman to the world for policies made elsewhere in the government.

Whenever he was called upon to make a public defense of the Johnson administration's Vietnamese policy, Stevenson maintained that the United States was opposing Communist aggression in Southeast Asia for the same reasons it had intervened in Europe and Korea. "The point is the same in Vietnam today as it was in Greece in 1947 and in Korea in 1950," he declared in the Security Council in May 1964. "The United States cannot stand by while Southeast Asia is overrun by armed aggressors." It was the familiar argument by analogy invoked by American officials during every international crisis since World War II. By 1964, however, the official line was showing signs of wear. While Stevenson continued to reiterate the standard rationale in his speeches, there is evidence that he was privately beginning to question these premises. On May 28, just one week after his defense of Southeast Asian policy in the Security Council, he gave President Johnson a memorandum which warned that "world opinion is simply not sufficiently prepared for either U.S. military action in North Viet Nam or a U.S. appeal to the United Nations." He continued: "There is grave question in my mind whether U.S. armed intervention in North Vietnam, consisting of more than sabotage and harassment, makes military sense. However, if the situation in South Viet Nam is so grave that military reaction against North Viet Nam is the only way out, much more political preparation is necessary." The memorandum observed that if the United States "can demonstrate clearly that it is Hanoi which keeps the Viet Nam war going, we can perhaps build up the necessary support for UN action or justification for U.S. action."[55]

On November 18, 1964, following Johnson's landslide victory over Senator Barry Goldwater, Stevenson gave the President another memorandum entitled "A re-assessment of United States foreign policy, 1965–70." It targeted Communist China as a growing threat to peace in the world and suggested that the United States should "shift the center of containment from Europe to the Far East," while at the same time seeking some sort of accommodation with Peking and better understanding with the third world in general. Giving a copy of the document to Vice President-elect Hubert Humphrey, Stevenson remarked, "It is so hard for me to find time to talk to anyone in Washington about the futures when there are so many presents—yes, and always so *many* present!"[56]

The two memoranda he submitted to Johnson in 1964 reveal that Stevenson had mixed views about the international situation. He was still a staunch anti-Communist, increasingly worried about China's intentions. But he also believed that "polycentrism or splintering in the Communist bloc and movement," as the November memo put it, would have profound consequences for the future. Accordingly, U.S. policy should be firm but not rigid, in order to capitalize on the ramifications of this "splintering" tendency. Stevenson's view of the situation in Vietnam was affected by this ambivalence in his thinking about foreign policy. He thought to the extent that China was "behind" the turmoil in Southeast Asia, the United States must continue to resist aggression there, just as it had opposed the expansion of Soviet power in Europe. Yet he feared that reliance on military force in Vietnam would create more problems than it would solve. Stevenson's thinking was influenced in this period by Barbara Ward (Lady Jackson), the British economist who was especially interested in the third world. She frequently sent him, at his request, drafts for speeches, many of which he used almost verbatim. John Bartlow Martin notes that Clayton Fritchey, Stevenson's principal aide at the UN, considered her "the single most important influence" on Stevenson at this time. George Ball thought that she was "a terrible influence" on him because Ball felt that her ideas were more facile than deep.[57]

Stevenson's dissatisfaction with the increasingly militarized nature of American policy in Vietnam is suggested by his involvement with a secret diplomatic peace initiative in late 1964 and early 1965. United Nations Secretary General U Thant sought to arrange talks between the United States and North Vietnam as early as 1963, and continued to do so into the spring of 1965. Stevenson took an active role in these initiatives, serving as a liaison between Secretary General U Thant and the State Department. It is not altogether clear whether Stevenson felt that these peace initiatives had much chance of success, but—unlike the State Department—he at least wanted the United States to encourage U Thant in his efforts to bring the parties together, either in a bilateral or multilateral setting. Harlan Cleveland has criticized Stevenson's conduct in this episode; he contends that Stevenson contributed to the misunderstanding by failing to fully communicate the State Department's skeptical views to U Thant thereby leaving him with false hopes.[58]

Stevenson sent President Johnson at least two extensive memoranda on the subject of Vietnam. These documents, dated respectively, February 17 and April 28, 1965, reflect growing concern over the escalation of the war. "I do not believe that we should pursue a harder military line with all the risks it involves without at the same time making it emphatically clear that we prefer a peaceful solution and that we are ready to negotiate," he declared in the February memorandum. He thought it advisable "to enter into some sort of negotiations soon if they can be arranged without unacceptable pre-conditions," for "as history shows . . . negotiations, after the agony of getting them under way is over, are themselves a *stabilizing factor* in the overall politico-military picture. . . ."[59]

But Stevenson's thinking was too deeply conditioned by the cold war for him to conclude that American policy in Southeast Asia was totally misconceived. Indeed, he shared the administration's view that North Vietnam and China were responsible for the turmoil in South Vietnam, and that the United States had to resist this "aggres-sion" in order to prevent a wider war from developing in the area. In his April 28 memorandum to Johnson he reassured the President on this point: "Our bold, determined action in Vietnam in the past three months has probably already persuaded the major Communist Powers that they can no longer pursue 'wars of national liberation' in Asia, even in a relatively covert form, without very grave risks to themselves." There is no reason to question the sincerity of this statement, although Stevenson may also have been seeking to dispel any suspicion in the White House that he was soft on the Vietnam issue. While he was gravely worried about the accelerated bombing of the North and the troop buildup in the South, he viewed with real apprehension the Communist tactic of using "wars of liberation" as a smoke screen for aggression. Perhaps Stevenson grossly underesti-mated the extent to which the fighting in Vietnam stemmed from indigenous problems, but so did practically everyone in the govern-ment at that time. At least he was a voice for moderation. Rather than relying exclusively on unilateral military action, he told Johnson, the United States should try "to tailor our tactics more specifically to the longer-run objective" of "creating an Asian consensus and eventually an Asian coalition for the containment of China . . . [which America] would not have to carry almost entirely on its own back."[60]

It was sounder advice than Johnson was getting from other sources in this critical period, but Stevenson's views apparently carried little weight in the White House. Two and a half months later he was dead of a heart attack in London. To the end he publicly defended the administration's foreign policies, but there is little doubt that he was privately discouraged by the direction of events and by his restricted role in policy matters generally. On June 28, 1965, James Wechsler, a longtime admirer, wrote in the *New York Post* that Stevenson felt that "a man does not lightly walk out on a major government mission unless convinced that conflicts over strategy have become irreconcilable issues of principle." The "obscure twilight zone," Wechsler noted, "lies between 'detail' and doctrine." In a brief but affectionate response, Stevenson told Wechsler he was correct in stressing the frustration inherent in playing "the constant role of 'debater' instead of 'creator.' There you touch the nerve with precision!"[61]

In December 1965, Adlai Stevenson III released a letter purportedly written by his father to Paul Goodman, one of the antiwar intellectuals who had met with Stevenson at the UN shortly before his death and asked him to resign. The letter had not been mailed before Stevenson died. It stressed the need to establish a "line" in Asia beyond which Chinese "expansionism" would not be tolerated, and defended the Vietnam intervention in this context, stating that "whatever criticisms may be made over the detail and emphasis of American foreign policy, its purpose and direction are sound."[62]

A communiqué from the State Department to President Johnson assured the President that publication of the letter to Paul Goodman "should successfully give the lie to the rash of stories" circulating that Stevenson had become skeptical about the Vietnam policy. But there is some question as to whether the letter accurately reflected Stevenson's views. Certainly it took a harder line than the memoranda he sent to the President in February and April. The draft was in typescript, with a few corrections in Stevenson's handwriting. Arthur M. Schlesinger, Jr., claims that Stevenson "did not personally write that letter and I don't know how much he really believed it." Schlesinger, Marietta Tree, and Clayton Fritchey, Stevenson's chief aid at the UN, all had the impression that Barbara Ward, who wrote many of Stevenson's speeches in this period, had drafted the letter . But she told Walter Johnson in 1972 that Stevenson had not discussed it with her. Whatever its precise origin, the letter to Goodman should be used with caution as a guide to Stevenson's views at this time. In 1970 his friend Harry Ashmore claimed that shortly before he died Stevenson remarked to him, "It is perfectly clear now that no white army is ever going to win another war in Asia. . . . That era is over. We don't understand that, and we've got to get the hell out of there as best we can." Subsequent events may have caused Ashmore to recall Stevenson being more definite on this point than he actually was, but it seems clear that by 1965 his thinking about American policy in Southeast Asia was somewhat in flux.[63]

7

In Geneva before the United Nations Economic and Social Council on July 9, 1965, Stevenson delivered what proved to be his last formal public address. "I take as the understood premise of everything I say that as a world community we are not developing as we should, and that our record of cooperation is inadequate, to say the least," he began. "But I believe, I hope, we can do better and that the nations meeting in 1970 will say: 'Ah yes, 1965 was a kind of turning point.' " He concluded with a plea for increased international cooperation in the space age:

> This must be the context of our thinking—the context of human interdependence in the face of the vast new dimensions of our science and our discovery. . . . We travel together, passengers on a little space ship, dependent on its vulnerable reserve of air and soil . . . preserved from annihilation only by the care, the work, and . . . the love we give our fragile craft. We cannot maintain it half fortunate, half miserable, half confident, half despairing, half slave—to the ancient enemies of man—half free. . . . No craft, no crew can travel safely with such vast contradictions. On their resolution depends the survival of us all.[64]

It was a fitting farewell address. The search for international community had been for twenty years a guiding theme in Stevenson's public thought. Through warfare both cold and hot, amid constant international crises, he stressed the need to build a safer, saner world order. His unique achievement, wrote Donald Grant in the *St. Louis Post-Dispatch*, "was to pull together the goodness in all men, the yearning for peace, for justice; to help all men achieve to the good life his brain and his heart told him was possible for mankind."[65]

In retrospect, Stevenson's later speeches have a predictable tendency, verging on staleness. Never an original or creative thinker, by the 1960s he had used up his supply of ideas. Meanwhile his thinking continued to be shaped by the premises of the cold war, his moralistic proclivities, and his belief in American exceptionalism. He could admit in 1964 that perhaps "the world was never as bipolar as it looked" a decade earlier; but he still insisted that, whatever errors had marked postwar American foreign policy, its basic purpose—the containment of Communist power—was sound. Without "claiming divine guidance" for the democratic system or "satanic perversity" for the Communist one, he told an audience in 1965, "I, for one, can see a difference—and can make my choice between them." While Stevenson had reservations about the specific means by which postwar American leadership responded to the Communist challenge, he never forgot the alleged lesson of the 1930s: that inaction in the face of aggression was the worst response of all. So he continued to defend the basic purposes of American foreign policy to the day he died.[66]

To many critics the Vietnam tragedy demonstrated the bankruptcy of that policy and the assumptions underlying it. Yet notwithstanding Vietnam, who can say with certainty that other policies based on different premises would have had better consequences for the world at large since 1945? To make such a claim implies an omniscience that Stevenson, at least, never claimed for himself.

"THE CHALLENGE OF HISTORY"

POLITICIANS HAVE ALWAYS found opportune uses for history, seasoning their rhetoric with references to the past in order to buttress their sagacious observations on the present. Winning votes, more than the elucidation of historical truth, is their goal. Presidential candidates often enlist the services of a politically sympathetic scholar to insure that their historical facts are in order. The list of distinguished scholars who at various times assisted Adlai Stevenson reads like a *Who's Who* of the historical profession: Julian P. Boyd, Henry Steele Commager, Walter Johnson, Arthur Link, Allan Nevins, Arthur M. Schlesinger, Jr. With their help Stevenson incorporated large doses of history into his speeches and, like other politicians, claimed it was relevant to some contemporary issue.

But Stevenson's interest in history went beyond its usefulness as a political device. While he was not a scholar by any stretch of the imagination, he thought of himself as a student of history, He knew it to be more than a collection of isolated episodes. Observing that the "whole lesson of history is its essential continuity," he sought to explain the importance of that continuity to the American people. For Stevenson, to talk about history was to confront the very meaning of American democracy. In this sense history was the ultimate political issue.[1]

In his memoir of the Eisenhower administration, Emmet John

Hughes recalls how he once gave the President a speech draft containing this phrase, "The world and we have passed the midway point of a century of continuing challenge." Angrily Eisenhower penciled in, "I hate this sentence. *Who* challenges *whom? What about?*" The reaction was "wholly characteristic of the man," Hughes noted. Eisenhower "distrusted abstractions" and "had found through the years . . . only one particular pleasure in history: the mental exercise of memorizing majestic dates . . . the more cryptic and elusive uses of history . . . provoked but a doubt and a frown." To Eisenhower, history was a record of facts, or it was nothing at all.[2]

Stevenson, by contrast, would have instinctively sensed Hughes's meaning; similar phrases abounded in his speeches. Whereas Eisenhower distrusted abstractions, Stevenson was comfortable with them. The "cryptic and elusive uses of history" were part of his idiom. For example, in a campaign speech in 1956 he concluded a sharp attack on Eisenhower's Mideast policy by declaring: "The search for peace demands the best that is in us. . . . We can no longer escape the challenge of history." Like Eisenhower, one is tempted to ask, Who challenges whom? What about? To explain what Stevenson meant, and what history meant to him, the best place to begin is where he began—in Illinois.[3]

1

He grew up in the Lincoln country in the early twentieth century, amid an upper-class family that took inordinate pride in its own history. His forebears had known both Lincoln and George Washington; his grandfather was Vice-President under Grover Cleveland; his father was a Democratic party activist in Illinois and an acquaintance of William Jennings Bryan. Stevenson relished telling anecdotes and collecting memorabilia about the family's history, which once prompted his estranged wife to remark caustically that the Stevensons "must have Chinese blood in them, they all worship their ancestors so." His mother never tired of reminding Adlai of the family heritage and of her high hopes for him. From boyhood, pride in family and country were intermingled, almost indistinguishably, in Stevenson's mind. He was also influenced by the patriotic tone of education in his youth. Stevenson was just eighteen years old, attending the Choate School in Connecticut, when he learned that a first cousin of his had been killed in World War I. Seeking to comfort his mother, he wrote her that the tragedy "should inspire in us all the spirit of sacrifice which alone can unite us in a general endeavour to maintain our countrys standards, which have so many times in the past proved so high." He noted that Choate had lost seven alumni in the war and had 136 men in service "which I think is a very good showing."[4]

From Choate, Stevenson went on to Princeton (1918–1922), where he compiled a thoroughly unexceptional record, both academically and socially. If anything set him apart from the other students, it was the fact that his mother also moved to Princeton and remained there until he graduated. Aside from this, by all accounts, he was a typical undergraduate, preoccupied with grades, girls, and football games, secure in the values of his social class. The prevailing political ethos was a serene assurance that America was blessed with a superior political system, which the privileged classes had an obligation to uphold. This ethos forever colored Stevenson's view of his country's role in history. In a fundamental sense, no matter how far he traveled, Stevenson would always return—figuratively and literally— to Illinois, to Princeton, to the certitudes of an earlier time. They reinforced his insistence that order and purpose underlay the movement of history, even as the tumultuous events of the mid-twentieth century jeopardized that faith.[5]

Thus when he spoke of "the challenge of history," Stevenson referred to the need to reassert American leadership in a world irrevocably changed by political, social, and economic upheaval. The world he aspired to lead as President was not the same one into which he had been born in 1900, as he knew perfectly well. Neither was the United States of America, for that matter. But Stevenson believed that the moral obligation of his country to preserve and expand freedom after World War II was, if anything, greater than ever before. "We in America," he delcared in a 1955 radio address, "are committed by history to a fighting faith in the power and destiny of free men in a free world." He insisted that the future of mankind— like the fate of America's own morally indivisible political system— depended on "living up to that faith and instilling it in others. . . . [because] no nation can isolate itself from its responsibilities to fellow men everywhere." Stevenson described this challenge in moral terms simply because he could conceive of it in no other way, and he maintained that the effort to uphold it must be a continuous process. Frustrated and alarmed by what he interpreted as national drift and purposelessness during the Eisenhower years, in 1959 he warned: "We inherited this freedom we talk about so glibly. We seem unaware that it has to be remade and re-earned in each generation of man." He said that he doubted "if any society in history has faced so great a moral challenge as ours," because in free society "there is no other alternative but to tap the vigor, the faith, the imagination of the people themselves."[6]

Admittedly there was nothing unique about Stevenson's view of the universal relevance of American democracy. Many public leaders and commentators were expressing similar views in the postwar years. The bloody struggle against Fascism rekindled the flame of American manifest destiny, and the cold war kept the fire hot. But perhaps no one made the case for American exceptionalism more eloquently than Stevenson. "Once we were not ashamed to be idealists," he reminded the 1956 Democratic National Convention. "We must dare to say again that the American cause is the cause of all mankind." "How far short we are falling of the radiant promise of mighty America, the child of revolution!" he exclaimed to the American Legion National Convention in 1956. "I do not believe that America's moral influence, or spiritual power, has run out, and that we can influence others in the world only by brandishing our military might," he asserted. "I believe that our best weapon is still the power of our ideals—the American ideals of independence for nations and justice for man—which are today animating Asia and Africa."[7]

The ideology of American exceptionalism has had profound consequences for the postwar world, ranging from the triumph of the Marshall Plan to the tragedy of Vietnam. Hard economic and strategic considerations, of course, have been as integral to this ideology as democratic idealism, but the idealistic element should not be underestimated. World War II spawned profound cynicism and doubt as to the very ability of mankind to survive on the planet. Yet the war against Fascism also revived a latent idealism in the United States— an idealism tempered by conviction that America's economic and military might, as well as its democratic values, was the best deterrent to another world cataclysm. While some leaders stressed military power, others emphasized moral resources as America's principal bulwark against Communism. It was Stevenson's ability to articulate the latter theme that made his words so appealing to many Americans. By constantly evoking the moral element in his speeches, he encouraged them to think that morality had been and would be the driving force in their history that he claimed it to be. He unabashedly brought the democratic idealism and moralism of the past to bear on the demands of the present. Believing deeply in the continuity of history, he assumed that the values which had sustained Americans in the past remained relevant to the new age born in the rubble of Berlin and Hiroshima.

2

When Stevenson needed historical support for his view of the importance of ideals in the American experience, two figures towered above all others in his mind—Abraham Lincoln and Woodrow Wilson. He portrayed both men as moral leaders who shared his belief in the universal relevance of American democracy. There was considerable truth in this characterization, to be sure, but Stevenson's depiction of Lincoln and Wilson reveals more about him than it does about them.

"Abraham Lincoln has always been my hero," he told an interviewer late in his life. "Bear in mind, however, that I was raised in Lincoln country. My great-grandfather [Jesse Fell] was Lincoln's friend and the first to propose him for the Presidency. . . . So I was naturally saturated with Lincoln from infancy." Lloyd Lewis of the *Chicago Daily News*, one of Stevenson's closest friends until his death in 1948, was a Lincoln buff and probably contributed to Stevenson's knowledge of Lincoln's life. Indeed, Stevenson had a complex psychological identification with the Great Emancipator. After returning to Springfield from the 1952 Democratic convention, he slipped out of the governor's mansion late one night and went to the Lincoln home and sat there for a while in silent contemplation. Several months later Stevenson spent a night at the White House; he wrote to Jane Dick that it had been a troubling experience. "Last night I finished with the President [Truman] about 11 & betook myself to bed—the Lincoln room & the vast bed. First I read a bit and then the trouble commenced when I tried to go to sleep—the ghosts and shadows that fill that room, bits and pieces of imperishable words that were conceived, perhaps written, here on this table where I am sitting—the very table on which he signed the Emancipation Proclamation after all those months of torment." As the night went on, Stevenson said, the portraits on the walls seemed to come alive, "The whole room filled with ghosts . . . and the portraits came marching up the stairs . . . or did I leave my room and . . . pass them all one by one? I don't know. But behind each in some strange dimension stretched out all the miseries, the burdens, the doubts and anguish that afflicted him [Lincoln] here in this house."[8]

Stevenson frequently cited incidents from Lincoln's career to support his own views on public issues. In November 1951, he spoke at Gettysburg on the eighty-eighth anniversary of Lincoln's immortal address. The Korean War was the dominant political issue of the time, daily claiming American lives and taxing the patience of American citizens who saw no end to the conflict. Stevenson used the occasion to contend that freedom itself was at stake in Korea, just as it had been on the line at Gettysburg nearly a century earlier. "Upon the fate of the Union hung the fate of the new dream of democracy throughout the world," he argued. "For in Lincoln's time . . . America was democracy's proving ground. The masses of other lands looked to us with hope. If our experiment proved successful, they too might win self-government." Still, "Lincoln's fight is not finished," Stevenson cautioned. The hills of Pennsylvania and the hills of Korea—1863 and 1951—were linked by a transcendent principle: "The fight [for freedom] goes on. Cemetery Ridge is shrouded in the mist of history. But American boys are dying today on Heartbreak Ridge far away for the last, best hope of collective security, of peace and freedom for all to choose their way of life."[9]

Stevenson continued to turn to Lincoln as a symbol of reassurance and hope in times of crisis. In February 1964 he spoke to the Abraham Lincoln Association in Springfield about violence in American life. President Kennedy had been assassinated in Dallas less than three months earlier. Stevenson himself had been spat upon there in October by anti-United Nations demonstrators. The John Birch Society was calling for the impeachment of Supreme Court Justice Earl Warren and demanding that the United States resign from the UN. Racial tensions were increasing. For his text Stevenson utilized a speech given by Lincoln in 1838, following the murder of the abolitionist leader Elijah Lovejoy. Then, as now, he declared, "Mad impulse, wild passion, hate and violence" were threatening the fabric of American society. "As the slavery struggle grew in intensity," he emphasized, "Lincoln maintained his stand beside Henry Clay and Daniel Webster, those champions of reason, moderation, and obedience to law." Today, as in 1838, he concluded, "The main enemy is not without. It is within—in the violence thrown out by social upheavel. . . . Now, as in 1838, we have not created our framework of liberty. We are inheritors charged with preserving a priceless legacy."[10]

The Lincoln with whom Stevenson identified was more the Lincoln of legend than the Lincoln of history, but to Stevenson the true Lincoln was indeed the Great Emancipator who incarnated America's commitment to freedom. "Lincoln was a man of all ages, of all civilizations," he reminded his audience at Springfield in 1964. "To-day, even as in his time, freedom and equality are the burning issues of a world in ferment. . . . The legacy that Lincoln left to all mankind is now the heartbeat of our time."[11]

Woodrow Wilson was equally important in Stevenson's mind be-cause, as he once explained, Wilson "showed us, on the world scene, an extension of what Lincoln preached; namely, that freedom isn't a limited—a parochial—matter, but a universal matter." Stevenson had met Wilson during the 1912 presidential campaign. Years later he reminisced about the encounter. "I was paralyzed with awe. . . . He asked me . . . if I was interested in politics or in public affairs, and he expressed the hope that I was. . . . I came away with the feeling: I'm his deathless friend. His supporter. His admirer. That's my man." If Stevenson was searching for a moral exemplar from the past, he hardly could have made a better choice than Wilson, the moralist nonpareil. In discussing Wilson's significance he invariably empha-sized how, in both domestic and foreign affairs, Wilson "contributed to a renewal of the American moral purpose." The dream of an association of all nations, working together to eliminiate the underly-ing causes of war ("dire need, hunger and disease, awakened hope, nationalism") was Wilson's enduring contribution to history, Steven-son contended. Although Wilson's League of Nations had collapsed and its successor, the United Nations, often appeared to be faltering, he insisted that history ultimately would justify Wilson's vision. "As Woodrow Wilson devised new methods to promote the common good among men and among nations," he declared in 1955, "so must we devise new methods to meet the challenges of our times . . . until at last the world will be truly safe for democracy."[12]

Stevenson's tendency to emphasize the moral dimension of Lin-coln's and Wilson's presidencies ironically raises a question about his own ability to govern the country. For it is not enough just to evoke the moral legacy of the past. Leaders must do more than that. The presidency would have forced Stevenson—as it forced Lincoln and

Wilson—to confront the fact that America runs on more than moral principles, sometimes on forces that have nothing to do with morality at all. The greatness of Lincoln and Wilson lay in their ability to recognize this fact and retain both their moral authority and political effectiveness. (When moralism overcame Wilson's political judgment on the League of Nations issue in 1918–1919, he suffered a crushing defeat.) Stevenson's record as governor of Illinois was by no means that of a fuzzy-minded idealist. Still, as other former governors elevated to the Oval Office have learned, the Presidency poses qualitatively different challenges. Stevenson as President might have risen to those challenges admirably. But since he did not attain the office, one can only say that his rhetoric dwelled too much on America's moral power and not enough on the practical exercise of that power. His view of the moral aspects of the Presidency was inspiring, but it was simplistic as well.

3

The subject of reform also reveals the limitations of Stevenson's historical thought. If the United States were to fulfill the mission he staked out for it, the first requirement was to clean up its own house. Stevenson knew that continued domestic reform was indispensable to the maintenance of America's reputation abroad. We must practice what we preach, he repeatedly warned, or lose our credibility in the critically important "under-developed" regions of Asia, Africa, and Latin America. Yet Stevenson's view of reform was also decidedly conservative, because he believed that history demonstrated that "radical" change creates more problems than it resolves. "Certainly there can be nothing more conservative than to change when change is due," he once remarked, "rather than to stand pat stubbornly until like King Canute we are engulfed by relentless forces that will always go too far." But what was the difference between desirable and undesirable modes of change? Was Stevenson's concept of reform as a preventive measure well suited to offer the American people an alternative to Eisenhower and "modern republicanism"?[13]

Some of Stevenson's critics on the left did not think so. While liberals almost unanimously supported his presidential candidacies, some of them grew unhappy about his cautious approach to social reform. Stevenson aroused dismay among many liberals in November 1955 when he told a gathering of Democratic leaders: "I agree that it is a time for catching our breath; I agree that moderation is the spirit of the times. But we best take care lest we confuse moderation with mediocrity. . . ." Ignoring the qualifying phrase, liberals jumped on his use of the word "moderation." Averell Harriman, who had presidential aspirations of his own, asserted that there "is no such word as 'moderation' or 'middle-of-the-road' in the Democratic vocabulary." Other liberals followed Harriman's lead; they feared that if Stevenson were elected he would abandon the cherished New Deal– Fair Deal tradition of bold social reform. The *New Republic* predicted, "If the Democratic Party has become the party of 'moderation,' whatever that means, and nominates a 'Me Too, Ike' Democrat such as Adlai, it deserves defeat and will get it." Although he endorsed Stevenson for the White House in 1956, Carey McWilliams of the *Nation* cautioned that moderation on social issues "will never carry us very far."[14]

The "moderation" issue was a tempest in a teapot, but it reveals how his philosophy of history affected Stevenson's approach to reform. What he was trying to do in 1955–1956, of course, was to win the Democratic nomination and hold the party together in the wake of the Supreme Court's desegregation decision of 1954. Some Democrats, however, felt he went too far to placate the South. Former President Truman exemplified their viewpoint when he remarked at the 1956 party convention that Stevenson "has always been a conservative, I think he was born that way."[15]

Stevenson in fact was "born that way," and other considerations besides the problems of the divided Democrats made him endorse "moderation." A go-slow approach to explosive social issues was the natural consequence of his background and was compounded by Stevenson's belief that enduring reform is necessarily a gradual process. He thought that the historical record substantiated his insistence that reform was the best means of preventing pressures from building up until they split society apart. It is significant that when Stevenson lectured on Woodrow Wilson at the University of Virginia in 1955 he appropriated the title of an old Wilsonian piece, "The Road Away from Revolution." In this speech he praised Wilson's democratic reforms for having prevented a more radical upheaval in America stemming from the inequities of late nineteenth-century capitalism. Wilson, he stated, understood that "poverty and underprivilege and the gulfs between rich and poor were fire hazards in America's basement." Wilson also realized, he declared, that poverty, envy, and frustrated nationalism comprised "the explosive stuff of international life." These were the problem areas which America must address in order to turn back the challenge of Communism and make the world safe for liberal democracy.[16]

With the assistance of professional historians, Stevenson maintained that reform had exercised an essential safety-valve function throughout American history. In a popular magazine article, published in 1960, he argued that whenever disruptive forces threatened to prevail in America, a spirit of "renewed attention to the public good" asserted itself. Sometimes, he noted, reform occurs "because evil has become so obtrusive that only vigorous action can check it"— as in the Civil War period. At other times, reform is a response to "subtler promptings," as during the Progressive era, when it was "disgust at the materialism . . . devouring America" which generated reform. But whatever the reasons for it, the recurring reform impulse reminded the rest of the world that "the American experiment has significance far beyond its own frontiers and is in some measure a portent for all mankind."[17]

Belief in American exceptionalism therefore was essential to Stevenson's understanding of reform. Like the liberals, he believed that the country should be constantly engaged in reform; like the conservatives, he thought that reform should be gradual, measured, orderly. He wanted the nation to have its cake and eat it, too. He desired to gain the fruits of social change without incurring the disruptions this usually entails. An idealized view of the past, intense moralism, and belief in the uniqueness of American democracy were the key elements in his thinking. America "is much more than an economic or geographical fact," he emphasized in a 1963 magazine article. "It is a political and moral fact—the first community in which men set out in principle to institutionalize freedom. . . ." The democracy he envisioned was a society which, while engaged in reforming itself, could reform the world in the process.[18]

4

Stevenson's belief in American exceptionalism had deep historical roots, extending back to the seventeenth-century Puritans' expectation that New England would become "a city on a hill," a moral example to the old, benighted world. During the ensuing three hundred years the vision of America as a city on a hill was successively reinterpreted by eighteenth-century libertarians, nineteenth-century imperialists, and twentieth-century Wilsonians. During and after World War II faith in American exceptionalism was associated with anti-Communism and the effort to create a new international order based on the ideal of American democracy and the reality of American power. Widely disseminated by various politicians, intellectuals, and publicists in the 1940s, these ideas formed an important part of the political culture of postwar America. Their impact on Stevenson's thinking was in large measure due to his association with people like Dorothy Fosdick, Herbert Agar, and Arthur Schlesinger, Jr.

Stevenson became acquainted with Dorothy Fosdick when he helped get the United Nations launched in 1945–1946; later, after his divorce, they had a romantic relationship. The daughter of Harry Emerson Fosdick, she had many connections with the American foreign-policy establishment. She sent Stevenson letters containing observations on political subjects as well as personal matters. In April 1951, for instance, she wrote him that "with the fate of the whole free world at stake," the United States must "rediscover our own revolutionary tradition." In this way, John Bartlow Martin has noted, she kept Stevenson in touch with the ideas that were circulating in official circles in Washington and New York.[19]

Herbert Agar was a journalist with a strong interest in history and foreign affairs. He helped to write speeches for Stevenson in 1952, including the one in Salt Lake City where Stevenson declared: "[The Founding Fathers] saw America as the old world's saviour, not merely in terms of power, but in terms of goodness. They knew that Providence had given us this empty, unexploited continent for a purpose. And they knew it must be a purpose which includes all men. . . ." In his book *A Time for Greatness* (1944), Herbert Agar asserted that "there is nothing worth fighting for except an idea. If the American idea is presently extinguished, the future will be dark for uncountable years." This conviction, born during the fire bombings of London and Dresden, from the bodies of dead and wounded stretched out on beaches from Normandy to the South Pacific, inspired the confidence of Agar and like-minded internationalists that a better world could be built only if the United States had the willpower to lead the way. With America in the forefront, all things were possible; without her, all would be lost.[20]

Arthur Schlesinger, Jr., enjoyed a many-sided relationship with

Stevenson: friend, speechwriter, historical consultant, political adviser. As noted earlier, in *The Vital Center* (1949) Schlesinger outlined a program for American liberals in the wake of the challenge of Fascism and Communism. He contended that the central issue of the time was whether Americans were prepared to strive indefinitely to preserve democratic values: "The struggle within the world against Communism and fascism; the struggle within our country against oppression and stagnation; the struggle within ourselves against pride and corruption [out of which alone] . . . can come the high courage and faith which will preserve freedom."[21]

The thinking of Dorothy Fosdick, Herbert Agar, Schlesinger, and others no doubt influenced Stevenson, but their ideas only reinforced his own deep faith in the special destiny of American democracy which had been implanted in his mind during his youth. World War II harvested what his family and education had cultivated: belief in the historical mission of the United States as the champion of human freedom. In January 1947, speaking to the Abraham Lincoln Library Forum in Springfield, Stevenson set forth his essential view of America's responsibility to mankind. "Just a year and a half ago we awoke from the celebration of the greatest victory over the greatest menace in history," he reminded the audience. "And we woke with the uneasy realization that our troubles had just begun—that what was finished was just an episode . . . in the headlong history of our generation. We awoke to discover that the world was restive, that there was a ferment of new ideas all about us, that the delicate balances of the old world had been consumed in the fire. . . ." But he drew a hopeful conclusion: "Our people are coming to realize, I think, that this generation of Americans can never relax. . . . We paid a ghastly price to learn that peace is indivisible, but we learned it for keeps. . . . If we have the statesmanship . . . tomorrow will be the golden age. There is nothing to fear save our own cupidity, shortsightedness and weakness."[22]

Although not an original thinker himself, Stevenson helped disseminate this creed as a presidential candidate and respected public figure. He fervently agreed with Herbert Agar's assertion that the postwar period was "a time for greatness," a time to demonstrate that the destructive capacity of American power which the war had starkly revealed could be subordinated to the constructive capacity of American ideals. As he told the New York Liberal Party Convention in 1956, "We cannot capture the souls of discontented people by boasting that our stomachs are full or our arms are strong. We can do so only by reviving the original American mission—the conception of our nation as the bearer of hope and freedom to oppressed peoples everywhere on earth." The "golden age" lay within reach, if only Americans had the wisdom, patience, and firmness to pursue it. But did they, in fact, possess those qualities? Even as Stevenson challenged Americans to fulfill their destiny, he wondered whether they would be willing to make the sacrifices he deemed necessary to attain it. The moral sensibility that underscored his faith in the country's mission also compelled him to worry about the character of the people themselves, upon whom his vision ultimately depended.[23]

To many critics of American society, its principal failure in the mid-twentieth century lay in the area of race relations. How could the United States claim to offer a model for anyone to emulate as long as it denied to Blacks their civil rights? The question had particular relevance for Stevenson because of his insistence on the morally indivisible nature of the American system. There is no evidence that the persistence of racial discrimination caused him to reassess his assumptions. Instead he relied on his faith in gradual reform to rationalize his contention that Blacks should continue to be patient and nonassertive about their situation. He thereby downplayed the moral aspect of perhaps the central moral issue in American history, and to that extent he embarrassed his own philosophy.

Stevenson's basic political position on civil rights was that the *Brown* decision of 1954 made school desegregation the law of the land and that all Americans must respect it. He maintained that time and education would eventually weaken the force of racial prejudice. He disagreed with those civil rights leaders who wanted to deny federal funds to school districts which remained segregated; Stevenson thought that in the long run it was better to keep the channels of learning open, even if the school doors remained closed to Blacks. When Senator Hubert Humphrey wrote him in 1955 about a pending education bill in Congress to which the NAACP wished to attach a desegregation amendment, Stevenson firmly replied that he disagreed. "I am convinced . . . that desegregation and improved relations are going to gain more from advancing education than from stubbornness," he told Humphrey.[24]

What Stevenson saw as "stubbornness" by civil rights leaders was more sympathetically regarded by some other prominent Democrats. "I do not know whether you appreciate what the word 'gradualism' and the word 'education' mean to Negroes and the White people who are deeply concerned with the civil rights issue," Herbert Lehman of New York wrote him in February 1956. Lehman was upset about remarks Stevenson had recently made in California when asked whether he favored using federal troops to enforce school desegregation. Stevenson said he did not favor the idea, explaining, "That is exactly what brought about the difficult [!] Civil War and division of the Union. We will have to proceed gradually. You do not upset the habits and traditions that are older than the Republic overnight." At another political rally he remarked, "The important thing is education. Things like . . . segregation will yield quickest of all to the spread of education." As Lehman pointed out, "It is difficult to speak of the enlightening effects of 'education' in a situation such as we have in . . . some parts of the South, where all the *active* education is in the direction of prejudice and discrimination." Stevenson underscored this last sentence and scribbled an emphatic "No!" in the margin of the letter. But Lehman was right in noting that Stevenson did not appreciate what "gradualism" meant to Blacks any more than President Eisenhower did. That is why many liberals were discouraged by his handling of the subject. "I have had, of course, very bad reactions from New York," he wrote rather defensively to Agnes Meyer. "But ultimately we have to face the fact that the ultimate sanction, force, will solve nothing. Meanwhile, I suppose my problem is largely one of attitude and the necessity for mingling more passion with my reason."[25]

In March 1956 he spoke at the University of Minnesota and again had to face the civil rights issue. Now he said that it was "a matter of grave national concern when a girl in Alabama [Autherine Lucy] is denied her constitutional rights . . . or when murder [Emmet Till] goes unpunished in Mississippi. . . ." But "against the failures," he insisted, "there is evidence that the process we have undertaken is certain to prevail—that we are managing to change the hearts and minds of men as well as the laws . . . this is the genius of our system, the means by which we see to it that social gains endure and enlarge." These remarks reflected Stevenson's conservative view of social change and his belief that history demonstrated the futility of drastic action. Hence his opposition to the use of force to achieve integration of the races. Such tactics, he thought, would only make matters worse.[26]

Meanwhile he received considerable criticism from persons who read history differently, who felt that Blacks had too long waited in vain for the fruits of gradual reform, who thought the time had come for more decisive action on the civil rights front. Voices on the political Right also began to make themselves heard, arguing that the federal government was pushing too fast on civil rights. Stevenson responded to critics on the Left and Right alike in a speech he gave in 1962 on the hundredth anniversary of the Emancipation Proclamation. Characteristically he relied on Lincoln to vindicate his own moderate position. "In his day, Lincoln was bitterly attacked for this unwillingness . . . to claim all virtue for the North, all evil for the South," Stevenson pointed out. He emphasized how Lincoln's "sense that issues might be relative and ambiguous roused men of rougher certitude to furies of denunciation, and Lincoln was accused of weakness . . . because he could not go along with the single-minded jingoism of much of the propaganda of his day."[27]

More than a quarter of a century after the *Brown* ruling, the cancer of racism continues to infect American society, calling into question Stevenson's faith in the ameliorating effects of time, reason, and education. The irrational element in the human psyche remains a formidable obstacle to the attainment of a more just society, as Stevenson acknowledged in his 1964 address to the Abraham Lincoln Association. "Ignorance is *not* invincible and malice *can* be exorcised," he insisted. He admitted, however, that he felt discouraged, not only by the violent acts of fanatics but also by "the silent indifference of so many enlightened men and women [who] in their hearts . . . condemn fanaticism, but . . . neither speak out to rebuke it nor take action to repress it." These words would have carried more weight had Stevenson himself spoken out more forcefully in recent years against the cancer of racism, but political considerations and his innate conservatism prevailed.[28]

6

As the postwar years advanced amid an avalanche of chrome-plated automobiles, electrical appliances, and other luxury devices, Stevenson grew anxious about the impact of the consumer revolution on the American character. Was the golden age he had envisioned after the war turning into a new gilded age? During the 1950s a Calvinistic tone increasingly characterized his speeches as he called on Americans to turn from self-indulgence to self-sacrifice. These speeches resembled the jeremiads delivered by New England preachers in the late seventeenth century when they feared that their forefathers' dream of a "city on a hill" was succumbing to materialism and greed. For example, in 1668 the Reverend William Staughton admonished New Englanders that through their sins they risked the loss of Divine favor: "If we should so frustrate and deceive the Lord's Expectations that his Covenant-interest in us . . . be made to cease, then all were lost indeed. . . ."[29]

Three hundred years later, against the background of a secular age haunted by the shadow of nuclear destruction, Stevenson sounded his own jeremiad to a society wallowing in creature comforts but spiritually attenuated. He was less certain than the Reverend Mr. Staughton that America owed its existence to providential favor, but he was equally convinced that the seductive lure of false values jeopardized its historic mission. "Your summarization [sic] of my anxieties about America and its *quality* was the tonic I needed for some utterances along that line," he told Eric Sevareid in 1955. "I keep thinking of great, jagged mountains melting into an even, molten mass. Is that what we are doing—in a high-powered, two-tone automobile?" "We can use our wealth and capacity for some vision of truth, some ideal of brotherhood," he affirmed in 1959, "or we can imprison ourselves within the selfishness of our own concerns and a narrow nationhood." If the latter course prevailed, he cautioned, it would be "a dangerous hour for our politics and for government by the consent of the governed. For at no time have so many of the great issues of the day demanded clear, real moral vision. . . ."[30]

Stevenson made these comments after returning from a trip to the Soviet Union in the summer of 1958. Impressed and disturbed by the dynamism and purposefulness of the Russians, he came home wondering whether free society could inspire comparable dedication in its citizenry. Following a visit to central Asia and Siberia, he wrote to Ronald and Marietta Tree, "This *is* the new frontier—booming, vital, confident and full of eager pride. It makes you *think*. . . ." Delivering the A. Powell Davies Memorial Lecture in Washington in January 1959, he said it was "impossible to spend weeks travelling around the Soviet Union as I did this summer without taking away an overwhelming impression of thrust and purpose in most aspects of Soviet life." He said he was not worried about American technology, science or physical resources, but stressed that he was "desperately concerned about our mainspring . . . the great central pulse of our freedom, the great truth of liberty, which, more than any other nation, we first set working in the modern world." Although Stevenson expressly denied that he meant to speak in a "Puritan or pleasure-hating spirit," the Davies lecture was virtually a modern-day jeremiad, a moral remonstrance against what he termed the "paralysis of will" in the West. "We do not slip into happiness," he warned. "It is strenuously sought and earned." The "natural government of man is servitude," he pointed out, emphasizing that only by "great effort, burning idealism and unlimited sacrifice" had freedom triumphed anywhere. But how could it endure, he asked, if the will to preserve it was lacking among the people?[31]

While calling attention to what appeared to him as alarming signs of decay in American life, Stevenson still thought that the United States could accomplish almost anything it wished, if only it had the necessary determination. "Ours is the first human community in which resources are so abundant that almost no policies lie beyond our capacity for purely physical reasons," he asserted. "What we decide to do, we can do. The inhibitions of poverty—lack of resources, lack of capital, lack of power—do not hold us back. We can accomplish what we aim at." Even in the process of criticizing the society, he shared the general assumption that there were few, if any, external restraints on America's ability to shape history. Perhaps "for the first time in the world, choice, not means, ends, not instruments, are decisive," he told the audience at the Davies lecture. What America lacked was willpower, not resources.[32]

Americans could reform history—that remained Stevenson's basic belief. But they could do so only by firming up the moral foundations of their society—that was his continuing concern. Like the Puritans, he contended that all external achievements of any consequence depended on internal discipline and ethical behavior by each citizen. "The essence of our material power," he reminded a University of Texas audience in 1955, "is a moral commitment whose maintenance against hostile pressures, and against our own inward corruption by the very power we wield, is our greatest mission as a people." A Calvinist tone also characterized the conclusion to his Godkin lectures, which he delivered at the old Puritan citadel of Harvard in 1954.

America's greatest contribution to human society has come not from her wealth or weapons or ambitions, but from her ideas, from the moral sentiments embodied in the Declaration of Independence and the Bill of Rights. . . . All through human history runs a struggle between right and wrong, which is destined to endure, perhaps, to the end of time . . . it follows that the solutions of our problems lie largely within ourselves, that only with self-mastery can we hope to master history. . . . Knowledge alone is not enough.[33]

No Puritan preacher could have said it better.

7

During 1959 and 1960 Stevenson began to speak out more frequently on the issues of the day, not only because he was interested in the 1960 presidential nomination but also because it seemed to him that the country was spiritually adrift. "Why are many Americans fearful that we have lost our sense of national purpose?" he asked in an article in *Foreign Affairs*. "Why is there confusion about intellectual and moral values? Why is there a slackness about public problems and a wholesale retreat to the joys of private life? Why is balancing the budget a greater national concern than exertion, self-denial and hard work?"[34]

One convenient explanation would be to blame it all on the Republicans, and Stevenson had no trouble giving the Eisenhower administration due "credit" for the sad state of affairs. In the *Foreign Affairs* article and elsewhere, he lambasted what he saw as the President's uncertain leadership, his inability to convey a sense of purpose to the nation. "Our foreign policy has been dominated by sterile anti-communism and stupid wishful thinking," he charged at the University of Virginia in April 1960, "our domestic policy by inflation and mistrust of government." The "essence of the task of leadership today," he proclaimed, "[is] to bring the nation back to a sense of its proper mission." Stevenson was particularly appalled by the administration's handling of the U-2 spy plane incident and by Eisenhower's having to cancel a state visit to Japan because of anti-American demonstrations. "I despair of stirring this torpid country into any sense of realization of our true position," he lamented to Eugene Rostow in June 1960. "Now with the Summit and Japan behind us, the signs should be unmistakable. But they are not! On the contrary, the usual soft music rolls out of Washington and Nixon gets cheers for converting our disasters into diplomatic triumphs." At the same time he told Agnes Meyer, "If we don't get a change pretty soon I dread to think of the further deterioration of our prestige and its implications for the future."[35]

Stevenson also knew that the national malaise had deeper causes than Eisenhower's faltering leadership, and that it was simplistic to blame it all on the Republicans. "Our own leaders have deceived us by underrating the magnitude of the crisis," he said at the University of Virginia. "But haven't we, as a people, also deceived ourselves? The harsh voice of history will be that our nation was quiescent and complacent, content with illusions." Uncertain whether the reasons for this condition were essentially political or whether they were deeply rooted in the character of the people, Stevenson turned to history in an attempt to put the problem in perspective. "Are we, in fact, as Professor [Arnold] Toynbee suggests," he wondered in 1954, "beginning the decline that has marked the course of all prior civilizations?" Depressed by the political vilification of the McCarthy period, he said that it "would be fairly easy to make a case in support of such a thesis." He cited as evidence the "shameless demagoguery and political expediency" and "the cynical exploitation of fear for political advantage" which seemed to characterize the political climate of the day. On another occasion he speculated whether the growth of "irrational criticism, abuse and mistrust" in American politics during recent years was symptomatic of "a moral and human crisis in the Western world," comparable to the collapse of the Roman empire or the decline of the feudal age; he warned it was imperative for Americans to "fill the moral vacuum" of the times.[36]

The demise of Senator Joseph McCarthy and the subsequent cooling of political rhetoric did not alleviate Stevenson's sense that all was not well with the American body politic. After his overwhelming defeat in 1956, he seemed to become more pessimistic about public affairs. Soliciting ideas from Reinhold Niebuhr in 1957 for a forthcoming speech, he explained, "What I had in mind as a possibility . . . was that since the explosion of the bomb nothing could ever be the same again." He told Niebuhr that "new thoughts for a new world" were "imperative," then added, "I sometimes wonder how long we of the West will even be heeded unless we lift our tired minds to originality and daring. But what originality, what daring?" In October 1957 the Russians simultaneously sent an artificial satellite into space and many Americans into a frenzy; Stevenson said the country "needed Sputnik . . . for it awakened in us while there is still time to remember the kind of people we . . . ought to be." To underline his view of the gravity of the times, he drew an analogy with classical history. "When Sparta was frightening the Athenians, Pericles said: 'I am more worried about our own faults than about the plans of our enemies.' And so am I."[37]

During the late 1950s Stevenson repeatedly urged Americans to demonstrate more self-discipline and take a more rigorous approach to the daily demands of life. In the preface to a book describing his 1958 trip to the Soviet Union, he noted that Sparta had defeated Athens principally because the Athenians "lacked the self-discipline to survive," and asked, "Is it happening again, right here and now?" He deplored how Americans "are frittering away talent, time and resources on trivialities—ranging from quiz shows to Detroit's chromium creations—while the Russians are concentrating everything on their overriding goal." He thought that the problem was "partly due to lack of leadership," but he also reflected, "I am not sure whether any President can persuade the country—without the stimulus of war—to do these things. Maybe our kind of democracy has a fatal addiction to short views rather than long . . . to private satisfactions rather than public necessities." That is why Stevenson said he welcomed the launching of the Russian space satellite, because it meant "there is going to have to be some belt-tightening, some more self-discipline" in the United States. "I suspect . . . that history is going to agree that this time of ours . . . was a time of momentous change," he predicted to a conference of educators in 1957. "The political process cannot, I am convinced, meet these demands" alone. Education must help; it must prepare students "for the shock of discovery that the world is in a tumult of change, and that you can't sit it out."[38]

The subject of education invariably aroused Stevenson's moralizing proclivities. Emphasizing the need for more challenging curricula in the public schools, he stated that while the Founding Fathers had resisted "external oppression," they "did not for one moment believe in doing away with discipline as such." He contended that only an informed citizenry, tested and hardened by the exactions of a rigorous educational system, could expect to meet the demands of the future. "If our educational purposes are unclear, if the curriculum is chaotic and cluttered with distractions," he affirmed, "our children will be educated for mediocrity." But what if, on the other hand, teachers and parents alike insisted on respect for academic excellence and restoration of vigor and discipline in students' study habits and courses? Then, Stevenson declared, education would serve "to restore the link in our children's minds between the happiness that is their birthright and the ardor, discipline, and responsibility that must lie in its pursuit. . . ." His educational philosophy was integral to Stevenson's historical thought. So that America might fulfill its mission, educators had a responsibility to cultivate values and attitudes that would equip students for the task. Stevenson stopped just short of saying that the purpose of education should be to indoctrinate students with democratic values. He believed in freedom of thought, to be sure; but the cold war caused him to look at education in terms of its ability to advance the national purpose. The best way to do that, he felt, was to reinstill some old-fashioned rigor and discipline in the classroom.[39]

Stevenson's educational views reflected his concern about the soft underbelly of postwar American society. Others who had similar anxieties sometimes confided their own apprehensions to him. A "creeping, all-pervading nerve gas of immorality starts in the nursery and does not stop before it reaches the highest offices," John Steinbeck solemnly told Stevenson in 1959. "I am troubled by the cynical immorality of my country. It cannot survive on this basis." Steinbeck's reflections were reminiscent of the remarks that Stevenson himself had made several years earlier about the ramifications of the gambling problems in Illinois. Like Stevenson, he viewed society as a seamless moral entity, wherein corruption at one level inexorably spread throughout. Steinbeck was working in England on a book about King Arthur; Stevenson said he agreed with Steinbeck's idea that the importance of the Arthurian legend was its "symbolism of the recurrent need in times of confusion and doubt for moral authority and direction." But from whom exactly did Stevenson—or Steinbeck, for that matter—think that this "moral authority" should come? From the American people, presumably. If so, from which ones? From those who were the proud heirs of the moral legacy of the past, or those who were busy buying television sets and second cars and joining country clubs? But were not these one and the same? In other words, it was the dual nature of the American character, its bewildering capacity to exhibit both altriusm and selfishness, that confounded Stevenson, alternately prompting him to make sweeping claims for Americans and to deplore their lapses from grace.[40]

He expected more from the American people than they were inclined to give in the 1950s. It was not a time for greatness, and no amount of willing could make it so. Too much of the growing middle class was too comfortable in its new affluence—and Stevenson was too quick to conclude that its conscience was forever frozen. Events in the next decade would dramatically demonstrate that ample moral fervor remained in the American character. "I say that young men and women should not be asked to accept the notion that the present state of things is the best attainable in our time," he declared in 1956. "There is too much silence, too much acquiescence, too little questioning these days." Within a few years young Americans alienated by the war in Vietnam began to raise plenty of questions about their country's moral posture. Sadly, Stevenson seems to have been unaffected by their protest, which was just beginning to make itself heard when he died in 1965.[41]

8

As Stevenson went about his ritualistic duties at the United Nations in the early 1960s, he took comfort in the idea that the UN had great potential importance in history. He saw it as a linkage between the present world of great-power rivalries and a future world of international cooperation. He thought his own era was one of transition, and consequently one of great danger. This fact gave the UN its significance in his mind.

The modern world was witnessing "the disintegration of one pattern of imperial power and the establishment of new political . . . relationships," Stevenson explained in one of his first speeches after assuming the United Nations post in 1961. Traditionally, he noted, such periods had produced chaos and war. While admitting it was "not easy to reverse the fatalities of history," he maintained that the overriding importance of the UN was that it sought to demonstrate that "men can live, not by violence and brute strength, but by reason and law." Speaking in Chicago in 1965 a few weeks before his death, he stressed the potential importance of the UN in mankind's social evolution:

We live in a twilight of power systems with few settled frontiers. We live in a time of growing misery for the many amid affluence for the few, and hence a time of potential international class war. We live in a time of acute ideological struggle.

Each of these has caused crisis in the past. Together, they

threaten catastrophe. What can we do about our triple crisis? Can we do anything about it? I will confess that I am an optimist. . . .

For man in his civil society has learned how to live under the law with the institutions of justice. . . . And in this century, for the first time in human history, we are attempting the same safeguards, the same framework of justice, the same sense of law and impartial protection in the whole wide society of man.

This is the profound, the fundamental, the audacious meaning of the United Nations. It is our only ultimate shield against disastrous war. Either we shall make it grow . . . or I do not know what . . . can save us.[42]

Stevenson spent his last years as a public servant arguing that nationalism had become both anachronistic and dangerous in the modern world. Any hope of progress toward peace depended on controlling the nuclear arms race and identifying "the ethical ideas which are the basis for long-range goals helpful to all men." To make this effort was not merely desirable, he told an audience at New York's Jewish Theological Seminary in 1961; it was imperative for the survival of the human race. "War is no longer rational, we say, yet the response to our mistrust of one another is more lethal weapons. . . . It is no wonder that this is the anxious age and that we want an ethic—an ethic for survival." He contended that the United Nations, for all its obvious weaknesses, offered the people of the world the only existing institutional means through which such an "ethic" might be identified. Because the UN had pioneered in the attempt "to establish some international ethical standards," it was "a symbol of hope for millions. . . ."[43]

Yet even as he lamented the persistence of nationalistic ideologies and outlined his vision of a new world order based on a common human ethic, Stevenson insisted that his own country was best equipped—by its history—to lead the way. Doggedly defending the universal relevance of the American political system, he remained at heart a cultural nationalist, convinced that any new international system must grow from the seed of American democracy. It was precisely the "vision of the open society fulfilling itself in an open world," he emphasized, that gave America "its universal validity." "This is a patriotism which sets no limits to the capacity of our country to act as the organizing principle of wider and wider associations," he said, "until in some way not yet foreseen we can embrace the family of man." Stevenson had no idea precisely how this nebulous goal would be reached. He simply continued to reaffirm his belief that somehow the fulfillment of America's manifest destiny was tied in with the evolution of a less dangerous world. Speaking in Dallas, Texas—a hotbed of anti-UN sentiment—in October 1963, he asserted: "As one who loves America, I wish to see her as a model for all mankind. For it is in America, I believe, that the fervor and will to create a more just and more coherent international order should and can be at its most enlightened and sustained."[44]

The same faith characterized an article published under Stevenson's name in *Look* magazine shortly after his death. Although the words were probably composed by someone else—perhaps Barbara Ward—the ideas were certainly Stevenson's own. "What we must attempt . . . is to extend to the whole society of man the techniques, the methods, the habits . . . upon which our own sense of citizenship is based," he said. "As heirs to the tradition of free government, what else can we do? Our founders had the audacity to proclaim their ideals 'self-evident' for all mankind. We can hardly be less bold when 'all mankind' is no longer an abstraction, but a political fact in the United Nations." Therefore, America must utilize "its ultimate vision and faith for a world society in which men and nations can be free."[45]

It is easy to dismiss Stevenson's thinking as visionary, simplistic, chauvinistic. Manifest destiny is not fashionable in post-Vietnam, post-Watergate America. Today we shrink from proclaiming our ideals, and with good reasons for they have been tarnished by the events of recent years. The American mission has been undermined by its own excesses at home and abroad. There can be no understanding of Adlai Stevenson, however, without an appreciation of the depth of his commitment to the idea of America and its promise for mankind. "Instead of being downed by actualities," John Mason Brown noted, Stevenson was "haunted by possibilities." His voice "had the ring of older voices," remarked Lewis Mumford, "the voices of Emerson and Walt Whitman, of Lincoln and Woodrow Wilson: it breathed the confidence of the pioneer and the conscience of the puritan." "My tiny world seemed suddenly to widen" when Stevenson spoke, recalled Richard Goodwin. "Events and the course of history were drifting back within the reach of a man's skill and brains."[46]

The words remain, but the speaker is gone—and so is much of the impact of his words, for somehow the enduring quality lay not in them but in him. In retrospect, Stevenson's ideas do not appear strikingly original or profound. Yet to listen to recordings of his speeches is to be transported back into an earlier age, a time when there was pervasive faith in the purity of American purposes and the universality of American ideals. Today there is a conviction in some quarters that the pursuit of those ideals has produced as much trouble as good in the world. But that is not what Stevenson thought. He steadfastly maintained that America had an exceptional role in history because he believed that Americans, for all their shortcomings, were an exceptional people: tolerant, generous, desirous of enlarging "the horizon of human hopes" and leaving the world a better place than they found it in each generation. And because he reiterated his faith in America so persistently and eloquently, he came almost to personify it. As Walter Lippmann wrote, Stevenson represented "the kind of American that Americans themselves, and the great mass of mankind, would like to think that Americans are."[47]

Are we that kind of people? It was Lyndon Johnson who said, "Adlai Stevenson believed in us, perhaps more than we deserved." Stevenson may well have claimed too much for us; he may have misread our history, misjudged our character. Still, he felt an abiding responsibility to protest the relegation of the American dream to its darker side, with all that portended for Americans and others. His America was nurtured on the Lincoln legends of the Illinois prairie, fired in the crucible of World War II—the product of a personal vision born somewhere in between mythology and history.[48]

AN AFTERWORD

ON THE TWENTY-EIGHTH and twenty-ninth of November in 1960, as the Kennedy administration was preparing to assume power in Washington, Stevenson talked with Soviet ambassador Mikhail A. Menshikov about improving relations between their two nations. Stevenson had met Menshikov two years earlier during a visit to the USSR, and he listened intently to what the Russian diplomat had to say. Menshikov emphasized to Stevenson, for transmittal to President-elect Kennedy, Soviet Premier Khruschev's hopes that disarmament negotiations would receive top priority from the new administration, because peace or war depended on finding a way to halt the arms race. While Stevenson was properly cautious about the Soviet initiative, he deeply desired Kennedy to make a serious effort in the disarmament field. Nothing seemed more important to him than reducing the danger of a third world war. One of the conditions he had set as a prerequisite for accepting the United Nations ambassadorship was to "be consulted about organization and direction of disarmament." In December 1960 he urged Theodore Sorensen to stress to Kennedy the importance of making an "unequivocal commitment to disarmament" in his inaugural address. "The main thing," he told Sorensen, was for the new President "to de-emphasize the bi-polar power struggle" and "to emphasize the affirmative approaches to peace." He sent along some possible draft paragraphs for inclusion in the address, including the following affirmation:

> We cannot be content to project beyond our frontiers little but rockets and the threat of destruction. We need to replace our human neighborhood of potential death with a full human neighborhood of common work and cooperation. We have only embry-

onic institutions in this field so far. We cannot allow our instruments of war to outpace the instruments of peace and construction.[1]

Stevenson may well be remembered in history only as a period politician who failed to attain presidential power—the William Jennings Bryan of his day. But in a fundamental respect his importance may be determined by the course of future events. As his efforts to nudge Kennedy toward substantive disarmament talks reveal, Stevenson was profoundly disturbed by the arms race and the growing danger of a nuclear confrontation. If anything, the danger is far greater today than it was in 1960. The nuclear clock moves inexorably toward midnight. Should the great powers discover a means of abolishing nuclear weapons and move away from the brink of disaster, Stevenson deserves to be hailed as a pioneer in the process, for he understood—better than many statesmen of his era—that the world could no longer afford to indulge in such lethal playthings. But if, on the other hand, the forces of destruction—whose strength he never underestimated—prevail, his will be a lost legacy among the ashes of civilization.

APPENDIX:

THE SOURCES OF STEVENSON'S PUBLIC THOUGHT

ADLAI STEVENSON TOOK exceptional pride in his speeches. His last-minute textual revisions were the despair of his staff during the 1952 and 1956 presidential campaigns, as he labored over sentences up almost until the actual moment of delivery. Hailed as a political figure of unusual integrity, he was sometimes credited with personally writing his speeches. But John Fischer of *Harper's* magazine, who was one of Stevenson's speech writers, has termed this notion a "genial myth." Like all public figures, Stevenson necessarily relied on other persons to draft most of his speeches. Indeed from 1952 onward he seldom wrote the bulk of any speech himself, and constantly solicited ideas and/or drafts from persons whom he respected. Some of those upon whom he called for help most frequently included Arthur M. Schlesinger, Jr., Robert Tufts, Herbert Agar, John Fischer, W. Willard Wirtz, Carl McGowan, David Bell, John Kenneth Galbraith, and John Bartlow Martin. Later, Barbara Ward wrote many speeches for him, and so did Archibald MacLeish and Clayton Fritchey. He often sought the aid of experts on a specific subject at hand, whether it was Benjamin Cohen on the hydrogen bomb or Professor Arthur Link on Woodrow Wilson. A good example of how he preferred to handle these requests is provided by a letter that he wrote to Herbert Agar in January 1956. Explaining that he must address the American Society of Newspaper Editors in April, Stevenson wrote Agar:

I have for a long time wanted to do something that might be called "The Image of America." What that is I am sure you know better than I, but I think of the impression which our country creates in the minds of people all over the world . . . I want to bring out the point that we deface the vision of America in the minds of people

133

around the world too often, sometimes by lack of understanding of our point of view, sometimes heedlessly and of late more often for reasons of domestic politics and personal gain. . . . If you felt you could find time to draft something for me along this line it would be infinitely helpful. . . . I see painfully little time ahead for the sort of careful thought and preparation which such a speech at such a time and before such an audience requires.[1]

Does all this indicate that Stevenson played an insignificant role in the evolution of his speeches? By no means. Conscientious and somewhat compulsive by nature, he tended to rely on writers whose ideas meshed with his own. Moreover he generally managed to add his personal touch to their drafts, a sentence or phrase here, a paragraph or more there, so that the final product had the distinctive Stevenson idiom. After detailing the extensive contributions of ghost writers to Stevenson's speeches, John Fischer nevertheless emphasized that "in a valid sense the speeches were his own," because the principal contributors shared his habits of thought. John Steinbeck once observed that as an author he could tell that Stevenson's words ultimately emanated from one intellect and reflected one style of expression, irrespective of how many hands went into their preparation. Michael H. Prosser conducted a study of Stevenson's speeches and concluded that he invariably stamped "his own character and imprimateur on what he said. . . ." William McCormick Blair, Jr., insists that there is "no question at all" that the public record accurately reflects Stevenson's views. Careful examination of Stevenson's personal papers for the most part substantiates this claim. Naturally he made certain concessions to certain audiences, but even amid the pressures of a presidential campaign he seldom violated his fundamental standards.[2]

When Stevenson went to the United Nations in 1961, he found himself in a different situation, however. As an official spokesman for the United States government, his speeches at the UN had to reflect policy made in Washington, whether he was in full agreement with it or not. These in-house speeches, according to Deputy Ambassador Francis T. P. Plimpton, originated in the State Department and evolved through the bureaucracy until they reached Stevenson's desk. Speeches that Stevenson gave outside the UN headquarters were more subject to his control, but under the pressure of business he tended to rely more than ever on favorite ghost writers for these occasions. Perhaps the most important of these contributors was the British writer and economist Barbara Ward, a personal friend who sent him numerous drafts that he delivered practically verbatim. For all these reasons, I have not made extensive use of Stevenson's speeches from the UN period, because their exact correlation with his own thinking is less certain than was the case prior to 1961. Yet many of these later speeches retain the familiar Stevenson flavor. Thus although his last formal public address—at Geneva, Switzerland, on July 9, 1965—was undoubtedly drafted by other hands, it still was a distinctively Stevensonian production, both in content and mode of expression. Within the limitations imposed by his position, he attempted to be true to himself to the end.[3]

NOTES

INTRODUCTION

1. *The Papers of Adlai E. Stevenson*, ed. Walter Johnson, with Carol Evans and C. Eric Sears (Boston: Little, Brown, 8 vols., 1972–1979), vol. 4, pp. 18–19 (hereafter cited as *Stevenson Papers*); *New Republic*, 17 November 1952, p. 5.

2. *Department of State Bulletin*, 9 August 1965, p. 229; Murray Kempton, "The Public and Private Mr. Stevenson," *Spectator*, 17 December 1965, p. 804; Irving Howe, *Steady Work: Essays in the Politics of Democratic Radicalism, 1953–1966* (New York: Harcourt, Brace, 1966), p. 222; *I. F. Stone's Weekly*, 26 July 1965, p. 1.

3. Jack Newfield, "The Death of Liberalism," *Playboy*, April 1971, p. 252; Joseph Epstein, "Adlai Stevenson in Retrospect," *Commentary*, December 1968, pp. 78, 83; Arthur M. Schlesinger, Jr., to author, 19 May 1971; Norman Cousins, "Does Anyone Remember A. E. S.?" *Saturday Review*, 1 May 1976, pp. 4–5.

4. Adam Meyerson, "One Virtuous Man," *National Review*, 25 June 1976, p. 692.

1: THE WELLSPRING OF A POLITICAL CAREER

1. *Stevenson Papers*, vol. 2, pp. 365, 366.

2. Ibid., vol. 3, p. 39; Mary McGrory, "The Perfectionist and the Press," in Edward P. Doyle, ed., *As We Knew Adlai* (New York: Harper & Row, 1966), p. 176.

3. *Stevenson Papers*, vol. 2, pp. 253–254.

4. Ibid., pp. 363, 364, 362.

5. Ibid., p. 29.

6. *New York Times Book Review*, 12 April 1959.

7. *Stevenson Papers*, vol. 2, pp. 456–457.

8. Quoted in John Bartlow Martin, *Adlai Stevenson of Illinois* (Garden City: Doubleday, 1976), p. 90 (hereafter cited as Martin, *AS of I*).

9. Ibid., pp. 319, 327, 335, 348.

10. Ibid., pp. 383-384.

11. Quoted in Kenneth S. Davis, *The Politics of Honor: A Biography of Adlai E. Stevenson* (New York: Putnam's, 1967), p. 206; Lloyd Lewis to Eric Seva-

reid, 16 December 1948, *Eric Sevareid Papers*, Library of Congress; *Stevenson Papers*, vol. 3, p. 233; ibid., vol. 6, p. 44; ibid., vol. 7, pp. 80-81.

12. Gordon Wilson Keller, "Adlai Stevenson: The Moral Responsibility of Power," *Humanist*, May-June 1967, p. 91; AES to Reinhold Niebuhr, 15 December 1952, *Reinhold Niebuhr Papers*, Library of Congress; Reinhold Niebuhr, "Liberalism: Illusions and Realities," *New Republic*, 4 July 1955, pp. 11–13.

13. Arthur M. Schlesinger, Jr., *The Vital Center* (Boston: Houghton Mifflin, 1949), p. ix.

14. Philip J. Scharper, "Humanist on the Stump," *Commonweal*, 19 June 1953, pp. 276–277; Thomas Woodward to AES, 8 March 1952, *Adlai E. Stevenson Manuscripts*, container 89-1, Illinois State Historical Society Library (hereafter cited as *AES MSS* ISHL).

15. Quoted in Martin, *AS of I.*, p. 524; Sevareid Broadcast Transcript, 12 August 1952, container 13, *Sevareid Papers*, Library of Congress.

16. Carl McGowan to author, oral interview, 6 November 1979; *Stevenson Papers*, vol. 3, p. 531.

17. *Stevenson Papers*, vol. 3, pp. 552–553.

18. Ibid., vol. 4, p. 5; ibid., vol. 3, p. 575; Jacob M. Arvey to author, 18 May 1971.

19. *New Republic*, 13 October 1952, p. 4; ibid., 11 August 1952, p. 4; *Stevenson Papers*, vol. 4, pp. 45–46.

20. James Reston, "Memo on the Two Presidential Candidates," *New York Times Magazine*, 24 August 1952, p. 1; Alonzo L. Hamby, *Beyond the New Deal: Henry S. Truman and American Liberalism* (New York: Columbia University Press, 1972), p. 281; *Stevenson Papers*, vol. 4, p. 63.

21. Martin, *AS of I.*, p. 755.

22. Arthur M. Schlesinger, Jr., "Stevenson and the American Liberal Dilemma," *Twentieth Century*, January 1953, p. 29; Richard H. Rovere, "Adlai Stevenson of Libertyville, Illinois," *New York Times Magazine*, 13 September 1953, p. 22; *Stevenson Papers*, vol. 4, p. 205; David Lilienthal to AES, 14 November 1952, *Adlai E. Stevenson Manuscripts*, Box 283, Princeton University Library (hereafter cited as *AES MSS* PUL); Gerald W. Johnson to AES, 12 December 1952, Box 282, *AES MSS* PUL.

23. *Stevenson Papers*, vol. 4, pp. 208–209; ibid., p. 206.

24. For extensive material relating to the 1953 world tour, see *Stevenson Papers*, vol. 5. The Miami speech is in ibid., vol. 4, pp. 327–333.

25. James Rowe, Jr., to Carl McGowan, 27 January 1954, Box 404, *AES MSS* PUL; Jacob M. Arvey to author, op. cit.; *Stevenson Papers*, vol. 4, p. 552.

26. Quoted in John Bartlow Martin, *Adlai Stevenson and the World* (Garden City: Doubleday, 1977), pp. 195, 211 (hereafter cited as Martin, *AS & W*).

27. *Stevenson Papers*, vol. 4, pp. 559–560; ibid., vol. 6, p. 4; AES to Archibald MacLeish, 28 April 1956, Box 435, *AES MSS* PUL.

28. Harry S. Ashmore to AES, 30 March 1956, Box 505, *AES MSS* PUL; Chester Bowles to AES, 9 July 1956, Box 426, *AES MSS* PUL.

29. AES to Arthur M. Schlesinger, Jr., 19 December 1955, Box 418, *AES MSS* PUL.

30. AES to Archibald MacLeish, 23 August 1956, Box 435, *AES MSS* PUL; *Stevenson Papers*, vol. 6, p. 210.

31. *Stevenson Papers*, vol. 4, p. 441.

32. Arthur M. Schlesinger, Jr., to AES (memorandum), 6 September 1955, Box 418, *AES MSS* PUL.

33. *Stevenson Papers*, vol. 6, p. 190; *Nation*, 17 November 1956, p. 421.

34. Adlai E. Stevenson, *The New America*, ed. Seymour E. Harris, John Bartlow Martin and Arthur Schlesinger, Jr. (New York: Harper, 1956), pp. xxix–xxx.

35. Bert Cochran, *Adlai Stevenson: Patrician Among the Politicans* (New York: Funk & Wagnals, 1969), p. 265; Midge Decter, "The Stevenson We Lost," *Harper's*, February 1969, pp. 98–102.

36. *Newsweek*, 27 August 1956, p. 17. It should be noted that the Democrats did retain control of Congress in 1956.

37. Quoted in Martin, *AS & W*, p. 399; *Stevenson Papers*, vol. 6, p. 375; Gerald W. Johnson to AES, 5 December 1956, Box 477, *AES MSS* PUL; AES to James Wechsler, 16 November 1956, Box 479, *AES MSS* PUL.

38. Quoted in Martin, *AS & W*, p. 406; *Stevenson Papers*, vol. 7, p. 47; the Oxford speech is in ibid., pp. 7–22.

39. *Stevenson Papers*, vol. 6, pp. 433, 532–533; Agnes Meyer to AES, 7 March 1957, Box 732, *AES MSS* PUL.

40. *Stevenson Papers*, vol. 8, p. 209.

41. Ibid., vol. 7, p. 367; Agnes Meyer to AES, 1 May 1959, Box 771, *AES MSS* PUL; quoted in Martin, *AS & W*, p. 476; George W. Ball to AES, 25 March 1960, Box 780, *AES MSS* PUL.

42. *Stevenson Papers*, vol. 7, p. 456; AES to John P. Marquand, 28 June 1960, Box 793, *AES MSS* PUL.

43. Richard P. Stebbins, *The United States in World Affairs 1960* (New York: Harper, 1961), pp. 28–31.

44. AES "Statement," 16 May 1960, Box 122, *AES MSS* PUL; *Stevenson Papers*, vol. 7, pp. 497–498; AES to Eugene Rostow, 17 June 1960, Box 797, *AES MSS* PUL; AES to Gerald W. Johnson, 20 May 1960, Box 788, *AES MSS* PUL.

45. *Progressive*, July 1960, p. 4; AES to Chester Bowles, 21 October 1959, Box 761, *AES MSS* PUL; *Stevenson Papers*, vol. 7, pp. 370, 430, 474, 475, 505, 515.

46. W. Willard Wirtz to author, 1 July 1971; *Stevenson Papers*, vol. 7, p. 510.

47. Quoted in Martin, *AS & W*, pp. 459–460; Arthur M. Schlesinger, Jr., to AES, 16 June 1960, Box 798, *AES MSS* PUL; Arthur M. Schlesinger, Jr., *Robert Kennedy and His Times* (Boston: Houghton Mifflin, 1978), p. 203.

48. *Stevenson Papers*, vol. 7, p. 507.

49. Ibid., vol. 7, p. 517; AES to John Kenneth Galbraith, 18 August 1960, Box 787, *AES MSS* PUL; Agnes Meyer to AES, 16 September 1960, Box 795, *AES MSS* PUL.

50. Quoted in Martin Mayer, " 'The Governor' at Work at the UN," *New York Times Magazine*, 7 February 1965, p. 88; *Stevenson Papers*, vol. 8, p. 429.

51. *Stevenson Papers*, vol. 8, pp. 189, 367, 495, 587, 601, 768.

52. Quoted in Mayer, op. cit., p. 88.

53. David Schoenbrun Broadcast Transcript, 14 July 1965, Box 14, White House Central File, USUN, Lyndon Baines Johnson Library.

54. Nat Hentoff, "Adlai Stevenson," *Village Voice*, 22 July 1965, p. 7. The most complete account of this meeting is in Richard J. Walton, *The Remnants of Power* (New York: Coward-McCann, 1968), pp. 172–179.

55. W. Park Armstrong, Jr., to Department of State (memorandum), 8 June 1965, Box 159, *AES MSS* PUL.

56. *New York Post*, 2 November 1960; Murray Kempton to AES, 2 June 1965, Box 898, *AES MSS* PUL.

57. AES to Arnold Michaelis, June 1956 (phonograph recording of conversation), Columbia Records #D25-793.

2: "A SEAMLESS MORAL GARMENT"

1. *Stevenson Papers*, vol. 3, p. 597.

2. Quoted in Joseph Alsop, "He'd Rather Not Be President," *Saturday Evening Post*, 28 June 1952, p. 118; *Stevenson Papers*, vol. 6, p. 219; AES to Murray Kempton, 21 January 1957, Box 729, *AES MSS* PUL.

3. AES to Gerald W. Johnson, 12 June 1958, Box 750, *AES MSS* PUL; *Stevenson Papers*, vol. 4, p. 129.

4. *Stevenson Papers*, vol. 4, p. 309; Adlai E. Stevenson, *Looking Outward: Years of Crisis at the United Nations*, ed. Robert L. and Selma Schiffer (New York: Harper, 1963), p. 254.

5. *Stevenson Papers*, vol. 3, p. 589; ibid., vol. 4, p. 206.

6. Ibid., vol. 2, p. 505.

7. AES to Brooks Atkinson, 6 April 1954, container 89-2, *AES MSS* ISHL.

8. For an excellent account of Stevenson's governorship, see Martin, *AS of I*, pp. 368–513.

9. Quoted in ibid., p. 488.

10. *Stevenson Papers*, vol. 3, p. 594; ibid., vol. 4, p. 124.

11. Quoted in Martin, *AS of I*, pp. 444–445; Adlai E. Stevenson, "Who Runs the Gambling Machines?" *Atlantic*, February 1952, p. 36.

12. *Stevenson Papers*, vol. 4, pp. 340–341.

13. The Progressive flavor of Stevenson's speeches was probably in part due to Arthur M. Schlesinger, Jr., an expert in the history of American

reform movements who helped to prepare speeches for Stevenson in the 1952 campaign.

14. *Stevenson Papers*, vol. 3, p. 173.

15. Adlai E. Stevenson, *Putting First Things First: A Democratic View* (New York: Random House, 1960), p. 115.

16. *Stevenson Papers*, vol. 2, pp. 471, 486, 528.

17. Ibid., pp. 558–560.

18. Quoted in Martin, *AS of I*, p. 6.

19. *Stevenson Papers*, vol. 3, p. 265.

20. Ibid., vol. 4, pp. 308–309.

21. Quoted in William Frank Zornow, *America at Mid-Century* (Cleveland: Howard Allen, 1959), pp. 70–71; Adlai E. Stevenson, *Major Campaign Speeches 1952* (New York: Random House, 1953), p. xxx.

22. *Stevenson Papers*, vol. 4, pp. 176–177; ibid., p. 52n.; Stevenson, *1952 Speeches*, p. 130; *Stevenson Papers*, vol. 4, p. 203.

23. James T. Patterson, *Mr. Republican: A Biography of Robert A. Taft* (Boston: Houghton Mifflin, 1972), pp. 446, 449: *New York Times*, 4 October 1952; *Stevenson Papers*, vol. 4, p. 22.

24. The speeches to the American Legion and at Wisconsin are in *Stevenson Papers*, vol. 4, pp. 49–54, 140–147.

25. Ibid., pp. 250, 253.

26. Ibid., pp. 426–427.

27. Elizabeth Stevenson Ives to author, 15 May 1971; *Stevenson Papers*, vol. 4, p. 392.

28. Martin, *AS of I*, p. 740; *Stevenson Papers*, vol. 4, pp. 166–167.

29. *New York Times*, 2 November 1954; ibid., 23 October 1954; ibid., 25 October 1954.

30. Stevenson, *The New America*, pp. 214, 249.

31. Ibid., pp. 277–278.

32. W. Willard Wirtz to author, 1 July 1971.

33. Adlai E. Stevenson, *What I Think* (New York: Harper, 1956), pp. xv–xvi.

34. Joseph Wood Krutch, "Reflections on the Fifties," *Saturday Review*, 2 January 1960, p. 8.

35. *Stevenson Papers*, vol. 4, p. 394.

36. Ibid., vol. 3, pp. 544–545; ibid., vol. 4, pp. 306–307.

37. Stevenson, *1952 Speeches*, p. 103.

38. Martin, *AS & W*, p. 323.

39. The alligator anecdote is related by Harry S. Ashmore in Alden Whitman, *Portrait, Adlai E. Stevenson: Politician, Diplomat, Friend* (New York: Harper, 1965), p. 284; AES to Gerald W. Johnson, 26 August 1955, Box 414, *AES MSS* PUL.

40. AES to Agnes Meyer, 8 February 1956, Box 438, *AES MSS* PUL; AES to Barry Bingham, 7 June 1956, Box 426, *AES MSS* PUL.

41. *Stevenson Papers*, vol. 4, p. 340; AES Speech to New York Liberal party, 14 September 1960, Box 124, *AES MSS PUL*.

42. *Stevenson Papers*, vol. 4, p. 16; ibid., pp. 524–525; ibid., vol. 7, pp. 524–525.

43. Ibid., vol. 4, p. 525; Stevenson, *The New America*, p. 192.

44. *Stevenson Papers*, vol. 4, pp. 257–258; ibid., p. 206; ibid., vol. 6, pp. 466–467.

45. Quoted in Martin, *AS & W*, p. 122. On the *Brown* case, see Richard Kluger, *Simple Justice* (New York: Knopf, 1976).

46. Harry S. Ashmore to AES, 2 August 1956, Box 425, *AES MSS PUL*; AES to Eleanor Roosevelt, 15 June 1956, Box 440, *AES MSS PUL*.

47. Stevenson, *The New America*, p. 245; *New York Times*, 4 April 1954.

48. *New York Times*, 8 August 1954.

49. *Stevenson Papers*, vol. 6, p. 118; Martin, *AS & W*, pp. 308–310; *Stevenson Papers*, vol. 6, p. 249; Martin, *AS & W*, pp. 369–370.

50. Quoted in Martin, *AS & W*, p. 369; quoted in Robert A. Divine, *Foreign Policy and U.S. Presidential Elections, 1952–1960* (New York: New Viewpoints, 1974), p. 151; *Stevenson Papers*, vol. 6, pp. 284, 286.

51. *Stevenson Papers*, vol. 6, pp. 278–279; ibid., pp. 280–281; AES to John Steinbeck, 15 August 1963, Box 867, *AES MSS PUL*.

52. Divine, op. cit., pp. 139–141.

53. AES to Dean Acheson, 8 December 1956, Box 476, *AES MSS PUL*; AES to Agnes Meyer, 27 November 1956, Box 438, *AES MSS PUL*.

54. AES to Eugenie Anderson, 27 December 1956, Box 476, *AES MSS PUL*.

55. Stevenson, *The New America*, pp. 218–219.

56. Quoted in David Halberstam, *The Powers That Be* (New York: Knopf, 1979), pp. 228–229, 236–237.

57. AES to Julian P. Boyd, 21 October 1959, Box 761, *AES MSS PUL*.

58. *Stevenson Papers*, vol. 3, p. 172; AES to Gerald W. Johnson, 21 January 1957, Box 729, *AES MSS PUL*.

59. *Stevenson Papers*, vol. 4, p. 39; quoted in Russel Windes, Jr., and James A. Robinson, "Stevenson Answers Twenty Questions," *Look*, 16 October 1956, p. 80.

60. Stevenson, *1952 Speeches*, p. xviii; *Stevenson Papers*, vol. 2, p. 571.

61. *Stevenson Papers*, vol. 7, p. 459; AES to Gerald W. Johnson, 21 January 1957, Box 729, *AES MSS PUL*.

62. Stevenson, *What I Think*, p. 44; *Stevenson Papers*, vol. 7, p. 391.

3: "STRIVING TOWARD COMMUNITY"

1. Adlai E. Stevenson, *Call to Greatness* (New York: Harper, 1954), pp. xi–xii, 1, 106–107, 108–110.

2. Quoted in Davis, op. cit., p. 91.

3. George W. Ball, "With AES in War and Politics," in Doyle, op. cit., p. 139; Carl McGowan to author, 6 November 1979 (oral interview).

4. *Stevenson Papers*, vol. 1, pp. 395, 425, 500, 522.

5. AES to Hamilton Fish Armstrong, 21 September 1953, container 97-4, *AES MSS* ISHL.

6. *Department of State Bulletin*, 20 April 1964, p. 619; Stevenson, *1952 Speeches*, p. xix.

7. Quoted in Davis, op. cit., p. 167n.; *Stevenson Papers*, vol. 2, p. 271.

8. *Stevenson Papers*, vol. 2, pp. 277–279.

9. Ibid., p. 279; Adlai E. Stevenson, "Lincoln at Gettysburg" (Manuscript), Rare Book Room, Library of Congress.

10. Dean Acheson, *Present at the Creation* (New York: Norton, 1969), pp. 3, 4; *Stevenson Papers*, vol. 2, p. 145.

11. *Stevenson Papers*, vol. 2, pp. 145–146; ibid., p. 245; AES to Samuel Levin, 3 October 1945, Box 237, *AES MSS* PUL; *New York Times*, 31 December 1945.

12. Michael H. Prosser, ed., *An Ethic for Survival: Adlai E. Stevenson Speaks on International Affairs* (New York: Morrow, 1969), pp. 75–77; *Stevenson Papers*, vol. 2, pp. 329–330; ibid., p. 359.

13. *Stevenson Papers, vol. 2, pp. 370–382, 397–405.*

14. *Ibid., pp. 400, 402.*

15. *Ibid., pp. 413, 431; Prosser, op. cit., pp. 119, 112.*

16. *Stevenson Papers*, vol. 2, p. 522; ibid., vol. 3, p. 175; ibid., p. 243.

17. Ibid., vol. 3, pp. 190–196.

18. Acheson, op. cit., p. 194; quoted in Martin, *AS of I*, p. 453; ibid., p. 454.

19. Stevenson, *1952 Speeches*, pp. 251–252; *Stevenson Papers*, vol. 3, pp. 470–471; ibid., p. 543.

20. *Stevenson Papers*, vol. 3, pp. 540–551; "Meet the Press" broadcast transcript, 30 March 1952, Box 6, Series 6, *Americans for Democratic Action Papers*, Wisconsin State Historical Library.

21. Quoted in Norman Graebner, ed., *Ideas and Diplomacy* (New York: Oxford University Press, 1964), p. 772; *Vital Speeches of the Day*, 15 December 1950, p. 157; CBS News Telecast, 6 February 1970.

22. Bernard Bailyn, *The Origins of American Politics* (New York: Knopf, 1968), p. 53.

23. H. Stuart Hughes, "The Second Year of the Cold War: A Memoir and an Anticipation," *Commentary*, August 1969, pp. 27–28, 32; "Meet the Press," op. cit.

24. Prosser, op. cit., p. 134.

25. Carl McGowan to author, 6 November 1979 (oral interview); AES to Philip B. Perlman, 17 June 1952, Container 89-1 *AES MSS* ISHL; *Stevenson Papers*, vol. 3, p. 576.

26. Quoted in John W. Spanier, *American Foreign Policy Since World War II* (New York: Praeger, 1962 ed.), p. 100.

27. AES to George F. Kennan, 30 January 1954, Container 89-2, *AES MSS* ISHL; *New Republic*, 14 November 1955, p. 17.

28. Stevenson, *What I Think*, pp. 69–70, 221–222; *The New America*, p. 27; *What I Think*, p. 224.

29. *Stevenson Papers*, vol. 4, p. 538.

30. Ibid., vol. 5, p. vii; ibid., p. 72; ibid., p. 427; Stevenson, *Call to Greatness*, p. 87; *The New America*, pp. 70–71.

31. AES to J. William Fulbright, 15 June 1956, Box 430, *AES MSS* PUL.

32. Martin, *AS & W*, p. 380n.; *Stevenson Papers*, vol. 6, pp. 280–281.

33. Dean Acheson to AES, 9 October 1956, and AES to Acheson 13 October 1956, Box 425, *AES MSS* PUL; Stevenson, *The New America*, pp. 29–30.

34. See Divine, op. cit., pp. 144–150.

35. Stevenson, *The New America*, pp. 34–38; Charles A. H. Thomson and Frances M. Shattuck, *The 1956 Presidential Campaign* (Washington: Brookings Institution, 1960), pp. 310–311.

36. *Stevenson Papers*, vol. 6, p. 361; AES to Dean Acheson, 8 December 1956, Box 476, *AES MSS* PUL.

37. AES to Agnes Meyer, 27 November 1956, Box 438, *AES MSS* PUL; *Stevenson Papers*, vol. 6, p. 407.

38. Thomas K. Finletter to AES, 11 February 1957, Box 726, *AES MSS* PUL; Herbert Parmet, *The Democrats* (New York: Macmillan, 1976), pp. 125–127, 151–161.

39. AES to Barry Bingham, 22 November 1957, Box 724, *AES MSS* PUL; AES to Arthur M. Schlesinger, Jr., 21 November 1957, Box 736, *AES MSS* PUL.

40. AES Diary, 25 November 1957, Box 734, *AES MSS* PUL; AES to John Foster Dulles, 29 November 1957, Box 726, *AES MSS* PUL; AES to Dulles, 5 December 1957, and AES to Dulles, 6 December 1957, Box 733, *AES MSS* PUL.

41. Thomas K. Finletter to AES (memorandum), 2 December 1957, Box 728, *AES MSS* PUL; Dwight D. Eisenhower to John Foster Dulles (transcript of telephone conversation), 3 December 1957, DDE Diary Series, Box 17, Dwight D. Eisenhower Presidential Library.

42. George W. Ball to AES, 25 July 1960, Box 801, *AES MSS* PUL; AES to Barbara Ward, 11 August 1960, Box 801, *AES MSS* PUL.

43. A copy of this lengthy document is in Box 790, *AES MSS* PUL.

44. AES to Barbara Ward, 28 October 1960, Box 801, *AES MSS* PUL.

45. Martin, *AS & W*, p. 563.

46. AES to Mrs. T. S. Matthews, 12 September 1960, Box 793, *AES MSS* PUL; George W. Ball to AES, 25 July 1960, op. cit.

47. *Stevenson Papers*, vol. 7, pp. 595–597; William McCormick Blair, Jr., to author, 24 May 1971 (telephone interview).

48. Stevenson, *Looking Outward*, pp. 157, 204–205.

49. See Martin, *AS & W.*, pp. 579–863, and Walton, *Remnants of Power*, op. cit.

50. Gerald W. Johnson to AES, 3 December 1961, Box 835, *AES MSS* PUL; Jane Warner Dick, "Forty Years of Friendship," in Doyle, op. cit., p. 286; AES to David Riesman, 3 June 1961, Box 835, *AES MSS* PUL; AES to William McCormick Blair, Jr., 5 December 1961, Box 829, *AES MSS* PUL; AES to Hubert H. Humphrey, 26 July 1961, Box 832, *AES MSS* PUL; quoted by Mary McGrory, in Doyle, op. cit., p. 178.

51. Stewart Alsop and Charles Bartlett, "In Time of Crisis," *Saturday Evening Post*, 8 December 1962, pp. 15–20; *Stevenson Papers*, vol. 8, pp. 351, 350, 352–353; see also Martin, *AS & W*, pp. 741–748.

52. *Stevenson Papers*, vol. 8, p. 347; quoted in Martin, *AS & W*, pp. 747–748.

53. Quoted in Martin, *AS & W*, p. 781; Harlan Cleveland Oral History Interview, Lyndon B. Johnson Presidential Library.

54. AES to Bill Moyers (memorandum), 14 June 1965, *Papers of LBJ*, President, Confidential File, Box 70, LBJ Library.

55. *Stevenson Papers*, vol. 8, pp. 554–555; ibid., p. 566.

56. Ibid., pp. 631–640; quoted in Martin, *AS & W*, p. 822.

57. Quoted in Martin, *AS & W*, p. 114.

58. Harlan Cleveland Oral History Interview, LBJ Library; Martin, *AS & W*, pp. 822–841; Walter Johnson, "The U Thant-Stevenson Peace Initiatives in Vietnam," *Diplomatic History*, Summer 1977, pp. 285–295; David Kraslow and Stuart H. Loory, *The Secret Search for Peace in Vietnam* (New York: Vintage, 1968), pp. 98–109.

59. See *Stevenson Papers*, vol. 8, pp. 702–705.

60. Ibid., p. 749.

61. *New York Post*, 28 June 1965; *Stevenson Papers*, vol. 8, p. 803.

62. *New York Times*, 15 December 1965.

63. WHSR (Rosen) to the President, 10 December 1965, White House Central Files, Confidential File, Box 59, LBJ Library; Arthur M. Schlesinger, Jr., to author, 13 July 1971; *Stevenson Papers*, vol. 8, p. 809n.; Harry Ashmore Oral History Interview, LBJ Library.

64. *Stevenson Papers*, vol. 8, pp. 814–815, 828.

65. Donald Grant, "A Walk with Stevenson," *Progressive*, August 1965, p. 5.

66. *Department of State Bulletin*, 20 April 1964, p. 617; *Vital Speeches of the Day*, 1 July 1965, p. 548.

4: "THE CHALLENGE OF HISTORY"

1. Stevenson, *What I Think*, p. 45.
2. Emmet John Hughes, *The Ordeal of Power* (New York: Dell, 1962), p. 18.
3. Stevenson, *The New America*, p. 38.

4. Quoted in Herbert J. Muller, *Adlai Stevenson: A Study in Values* (New York: Harper, 1967), p. 25; *Stevenson Papers,* vol. 1, p. 49.

5. See Martin, *AS of I,* pp. 55–58.

6. Stevenson, *What I Think,* p. 170; *Putting First Things First* (New York: Random House, 1960), pp. 33, 37.

7. Stevenson, *The New America,* p. 9; AES Address to the American Legion, 5 September 1956, Box 92, *AES MSS* PUL.

8. Quoted in Lillian Ross, *Adlai Stevenson* (Philadelphia: Lippincott, 1966), pp. 55–56; *Stevenson Papers,* vol. 4, p. 213.

9. *Stevenson Papers,* vol. 3, pp. 469–471.

10. Ibid., vol. 8, pp. 511–512, 515.

11. Ibid., p. 510.

12. Quoted in Ross, op. cit., pp. 56–57; *Stevenson Papers,* vol. 4, pp. 586, 590–591.

13. Quoted in Joseph Epstein, "Adlai Stevenson in Retrospect," *Commentary,* December 1968, p. 77.

14. *Stevenson Papers,* vol. 6, p. 9; ibid.; *New Republic,* 21 May 1956, p. 23; *Nation,* 25 August 1956, p. 151.

15. Quoted in *New Republic,* 27 August 1956, p. 3.

16. *Stevenson Papers,* vol. 4, pp. 585–587. Professor Arthur Link, the foremost Wilsonian scholar, helped to prepare this speech.

17. Adlai E. Stevenson, " 'Extend our Vision . . . all Mankind,' " *Life,* 30 May 1960, p. 94.

18. Adlai E. Stevenson, "The Hard Kind of Patriotism," *Harper's,* July 1963, p. 32.

19. Martin, *AS of I,* pp. 474–476.

20. *Stevenson Papers,* vol. 4, p. 160; Herbert Agar, *A Time for Greatness* (Boston: Little, Brown, 1944), pp. 300–301.

21. Schlesinger, *Vital Center,* p. 256.

22. *Stevenson Papers,* vol. 2, pp. 370–371, 382.

23. Stevenson, *The New America,* p. 217.

24. *Stevenson Papers,* vol. 4, p. 528.

25. Herbert Lehman to AES, 11 February 1956, Box 435, *AES MSS* PUL; Martin, *AS & W,* pp. 258–267; AES to Agnes Meyer, 20 February 1956, Box 438, *AES MSS* PUL.

26. AES Address, University of Minnesota, 2 March 1956, Box 118, *AES MSS* PUL.

27. *Stevenson Papers,* vol. 8, p. 293.

28. Ibid., pp. 512, 515.

29. Quoted in Perry Miller, *Errand into the Wilderness* (New York: Harper, 1964), p. 6.

30. *Stevenson Papers,* vol. 6, p. 16; ibid., vol. 7, p. 332.

31. Ibid., vol. 7, p. 250; ibid., pp. 323, 325–327.

32. Ibid., p. 328.

33. Ibid., vol. 5, pp. 488–489.

34. Stevenson, *First Things First*, pp. 3–4.

35. *Stevenson Papers*, vol. 7, pp. 457, 456; AES to Eugene Rostow, 24 June 1960, Box 797, *AES MSS* PUL; AES to Agnes Meyer, 21 June 1960, Box 795, *AES MSS* PUL.

36. *Stevenson Papers*, vol. 7, p. 457; Adlai E. Stevenson, "Must We Have War?" *Look*, 16 November 1954, p. 54; *Vital Speeches of the Day*, 1 July 1954, p. 551.

37. AES to Reinhold Niebuhr, 23 January 1957, *Niebuhr Papers*, op cit.; *Vital Speeches of the Day*, 15 December 1957, p. 134.

38. Adlai E. Stevenson, *Friends and Enemies* (New York: Harper, 1959), pp. xx–xxii; AES Address, Chapel Hill, North Carolina, 28 September 1957, Box 115, *AES MSS* PUL.

39. Adlai E. Stevenson, "Dual Education Problem: School and Home," *New York Times Magazine*, 6 April 1958, p. 65; Chapel Hill Address, op. cit.; "Dual Education," p. 65.

40. John Steinbeck to AES, 5 November 1959, Box 776, *AES MSS* PUL; "Our 'Rigged' Morality," *Coronet*, March 1960, p. 146.

41. AES, "Message to Students" (transcript of radio broadcast), 25 October 1956, Box 99, *AES MSS* PUL.

42. *Department of State Bulletin*, 20 March 1961, pp. 411, 413; *Vital Speeches of the Day*, 1 August 1965, p. 617.

43. *Stevenson Papers*, vol. 8, pp. 61–65.

44. Stevenson, "Hard Patriotism," p. 34; *Vital Speeches of the Day*, 15 November 1963, p. 71.

45. "Adlai Stevenson's Last Article: Outline for a New American Policy," *Look*, 24 August 1956, p. 81.

46. John Mason Brown, *Through These Men* (New York: Harper, 1956); *New Republic*, 4 August 1952, p. 3; Richard Goodwin, *The Sower's Seed: A Tribute to Adlai Stevenson* (New American Library, 1965), pp. 11, 13.

47. *New York Herald Tribune*, 20 July 1965.

48. Quoted in Whitman, *Portrait*, op. cit., p. 269.

AN AFTERWORD

1. *Stevenson Papers*, vol. 7, pp. 587–591, 597, 604–605, 608.

Appendix

1. John Fischer, "A Footnote on Adlai E. Stevenson," *Harper's*, November 1965, p. 20; *Stevenson Papers*, vol. 6, pp. 41–42.

2. Fischer, op. cit., p. 23; Prosser, op. cit., p. 32; William McCormick Blair, Jr., to author (oral interview), 7 April 1972.

3. *Stevenson Papers*, vol. 8, p. xix.

SELECTED BIBLIOGRAPHY

1. Manuscript Collections

All the following collections were useful, but the Adlai E. Stevenson Papers at Princeton University, superbly catalogued and accessible despite the enormous size of the collection, were by far the most important for my purposes. While much of this material has been published in Walter Johnson's edition of the Stevenson Papers, there is no substitute for working through the documents themselves. The Stevenson Gubernatorial Papers at the Illinois State Historical Society were less useful, but did contain some important correspondence covering the years 1949–1956. After Stevenson took up the United Nations ambassadorship in 1961, his personal correspondence became much less rich, presumably because the pressure of his duties prevented him from writing to friends as frequently as he had done in the past. But the Princeton and Illinois collections contain invaluable letters from the 1940s and 1950s, as well as countless manuscripts of speeches, transcripts of interviews, and clippings.

Dwight D. Eisenhower Presidential Library, Abilene, Kansas:
    Dwight D.Eisenhower Papers
                DDE Diary Series
                DDE Personal Papers (Ann Whitman File)

Illinois State Historical Society Library, Springfield, Illinois:
    Adlai E. Stevenson Papers (Gubernatorial and Selected Correspondence)

Lyndon B. Johnson Presidential Library, Austin, Texas:
    Lyndon B. Johnson Papers
        LBJ, Famous Name File
        LBJ, Senate File
        LBJ, President, Confidential File
        National Security File
        White House Central File, International Organizations
        (United Nations)

Library of Congress, Washington, D.C.:
  Eric Sevareid Papers
  Reinhold Niebuhr Papers

Princeton University Library:
  Adlai E. Stevenson Papers

Harry S. Truman Presidential Library, Independence, Missouri:
  Will Clayton Papers
  Stephen A. Mitchell Papers
  Charles S. Murphy Papers
  Harry S. Truman Papers
    Official File (White House)
    Post-Presidential File

Wisconsin State Historical Society Library, Madison, Wisconsin:
  Americans for Democratic Action Papers
  John Fischer Papers
  Newton N. Minow Papers
  Dore Schary Papers

2. Oral History Collections
  The Columbia University Oral History Project contains a large Stevenson collection, but the most important interviews therein are closed. The following oral history transcripts were useful:
  Harry Ashmore, Lyndon B. Johnson Presidential Library
  Samuel C. Brightman, Harry S. Truman Library
  Harlan Cleveland, Lyndon B. Johnson Presidential Library
  Chester Cooper, Lyndon B. Johnson Presidential Library
  Eric Hodgins, Columbia University Oral History Project (copy in Eisenhower Library)
  Carl McGowan, Harry S. Truman Library
  Richard H. Rovere, Columbia University Oral History Project (copy in Eisenhower Library)
  James L. Sundquist, Harry S. Truman Library

3. Published Writings by Adlai E. Stevenson.
  At one time or another during his life, Stevenson wrote for numerous magazines and his speeches were widely reproduced in many places. The easiest, surest way to survey his thought, public and private, is to go to *The Papers of Adlai E. Stevenson*, edited by Walter Johnson, with Carol Evans and C. Eric Sears, 8 vols. (Boston: Little, Brown and Co., 1972–1979). It is remarkable to see a thorough edition of a person's writings published within a few years of his death. Naturally Johnson had to defer to the Stevenson family's wishes and delete items or passages that might have embarrassed

living persons. Nevertheless, the edition is for the most part a judicious, revealing collection. The principal criticism which can be made of it is that so many pages are devoted to Stevenson's 1953 world tour—a disproportionate emphasis in my view.

Besides the *Papers*, the following published collections of Stevenson's writings and speeches were helpful:

Michael H. Prosser (ed.), *An Ethic for Survival: Adlai E. Stevenson Speaks on International Affairs, 1936–1965*. New York: William Morrow, 1969.

Adlai E. Stevenson, *The Alliance for Progress*. Department of State, 1961.

———, *Call to Greatness*. New York: Harper & Brothers, 1954.

———, *Friends and Enemies: What I Learned in Russia*. New York: Harper & Brothers, 1959.

———, *Looking Outward: Years of Crisis at the United Nations*, ed. by Robert L. and Selma Schiffer. New York: Harper & Row, 1963.

———, *Major Campaign Speeches of Adlai E. Stevenson, 1952*. New York: Random House, 1953.

———, *The New America*, ed. Seymour E. Harris, John Bartlow Martin, and Arthur Schlesinger, Jr. New York: Harper & Brothers, 1957.

———, *Putting First Things First: A Democratic View*. New York: Random House, 1960.

———, *What I Think*. New York: Harper & Brothers, 1956.

4. Magazines

Rather than endeavoring to list each relevant item separately, I have simply itemized those periodicals that I found most valuable. For specific references, see the notes for each chapter.

Commentary; Foreign Affairs; I. F. Stone's Weekly; Nation; New Republic; New Yorker; Progressive; Reporter; Saturday Review; Vital Speeches.

5. Books

One could go on indefinitely listing relevant monographs, biographies, memoirs, texts, etc. I have cited only those books that were of major help to me in one way or another.

It may be worthwhile to consider the various biographies of Stevenson separately. By far the best—in scope, depth, judiciousness, perceptiveness— is John Bartlow Martin's two-volume study, *Adlai Stevenson of Illinois* (Garden City: Doubleday & Co., 1976) and *Adlai Stevenson and the World* (Garden City: Doubleday & Co., 1977). Shortly after Stevenson died, his family commissioned Martin to write the authorized study. He produced an exhaustive portrait of Stevenson and his times. Perhaps the major importance of the work is its contribution to our knowledge of Stevenson's personal life after the divorce and its insights into the 1952 and 1956 presidential campaigns. As an associate of Stevenson's, Martin has an invaluable perspective. Though understandably favorable, the work is not blatantly biased toward its subject—Stevenson's warts, as well as his virtues, come through. The major weakness of Martin's study is that the very wealth of detail, which is also its strength at times makes it difficult to distinguish the relevant from the irrelevant. Keen insights often get lost in the process. Professional scholars will find Martin's study inadequate in terms of historical perspective and unoriginal when it does make historical judgments. But Martin is not a professional historian, and he should not be criticized except in terms of what he set out to do. On this basis, he did a good job with a difficult subject. There is a certain elusive quality to Adlai Stevenson that defies definitive explanation.

Martin's biography has supplanted all previous studies of Stevenson, but one of them still merits attention: Bert Cochran, *Adlai Stevenson: Patrician Among the Politicians* (New York: Funk & Wagnalls, 1969). Cochran was the first biographer to bring a critical perspective to Stevenson's career. Another perceptive assessment is Joseph Epstein, "Adlai Stevenson in Retrospect," *Commentary*, December 1968, pp. 71–83.

As far as other monographs are concerned, the following books, in one way or another, helped me to write this one:

Acheson, Dean. *Present at the Creation*. New York: W. W. Norton, 1969.

Adler, Selig. *The Isolationist Impulse: Its Twentieth Century Reaction*. New York: Abelard-Schuman, 1957.

Agar, Herbert. *A Time for Greatness*. Boston: Little, Brown and Co., 1944.

———. *The Price of Power*. Chicago: University of Chicago Press, 1957.

Anderson, Clinton P., with Milton Viorst. *Outsider in the Senate*. New York: World Publishing Company, 1970.

Bailyn, Bernard. *The Origins of American Politics*. New York: Alfred A. Knopf, 1968.

Bernstein, Barton J., ed. *Politics and Policies of the Truman Administration*. Chicago: Quadrangle Books, 1970.

Bernstein, Barton J. "Election of 1952," in Arthur M. Schlesinger, Jr., ed., *The Coming to Power: Critical Presidential Elections in American History*. New York: Chelsea House Publishers, 1971.

Brown, John Mason. *Through These Men*. New York: Harper & Brothers, 1956.

Brown, Stuart Garry. *Conscience in Politics: Adlai E. Stevenson in the 1950s*. Syracuse: Syracuse University Press, 1961.

Davis, Kenneth S. *The Politics of Honor: A Biography of Adlai E. Stevenson*. New York: G. P. Putnam's Sons, 1967.

Divine, Robert A. *Foreign Policy and U.S. Presidential Elections, 1952–1960*. New York: New Viewpoints, 1974.

Doyle, Edward P., ed. *As We Knew Adlai*. New York: Harper & Row, 1966.

Goldman, Eric. *The Crucial Decade—and After*. New York: Vintage, 1960.

Goodwin, Richard N. *The Sower's Seed: A Tribute to Adlai Stevenson*. New York: New American Library, 1965.

Gorman, Joseph Bruce. *Kefauver: A Political Biography*. New York: Oxford University Press, 1971.

Halberstam, David. *The Powers That Be*. New York: Alfred A. Knopf, 1979.

Hamby, Alonzo L. *Beyond the New Deal: Harry S. Truman and American Liberalism*. New York: Columbia University Press, 1971.

Hofstadter, Richard. *Anti-intellectualism in American Life*. New York: Alfred A. Knopf, 1963.

Howe, Irving. *Steady Work: Essays in the Politics of Democratic Radicalism, 1953–1966*. New York: Harcourt, Brace and World, 1966.

Hughes, Emmet John. *The Ordeal of Power*. New York: Dell Books, 1964.

Johnson, Walter. *How We Drafted Adlai Stevenson*. New York: Alfred A. Knopf, 1955.

Kennedy, Robert F. *Thirteen Days: A Memoir of the Cuban Missile Crisis*. New York: New American Library, 1969.

Kraslow, David, and Stuart H. Loory. *The Secret Search for Peace in Vietnam*. New York: Vintage Books, 1968.

Lippmann, Walter. "Preface" to *Adlai Stevenson's Public Years*, ed. by Jill Kneerim. New York: Grossman Publishers, 1966.

Lubell, Samuel. *Revolt of the Moderates*. New York: Harper & Brothers, 1956.

Muller, Herbert J. *Adlai Stevenson: A Study in Values*. New York: Harper & Row, 1967.

Parmet, Herbert S. *The Democrats: The Years After FDR*. New York: Macmillan Co., 1976.

Patterson, James T. *Mr. Republican: A Biography of Robert A. Taft*. Boston: Houghton Mifflin Co., 1972.

Potter, David M. *People of Plenty: Economic Abundance and the American Character*. Chicago: University of Chicago Press, 1954.

Ross, Lillian. *Adlai Stevenson*. Philadelphia: J. B. Lippincott Co., 1966.

Schlesinger, Arthur M., Jr. *Robert Kennedy and His Times*. Boston: Houghton Mifflin Co., 1978.

Schlesinger, Arthur M., Jr. *A Thousand Days*. New York: Fawcett Books, 1965.

Spanier, John W. *American Foreign Policy Since World War II*. New York: Frederick A. Praeger, 1962.

Stebbins, Richard P. *The United States in World Affairs 1960*. New York: Harper & Brothers, 1961.

Thomson, Charles A. H., and Frances M. Shattuck. *The 1956 Presidential Campaign*. Washington: Brookings Institution, 1960.

Tillett, Paul, ed. *Inside Politics: The National Conventions, 1960*. Dobbs Ferry, New York: 1962.

Trilling, Lionel. *The Liberal Imagination*. New York: Viking Press, 1950.

Walton, Richard J. *The Remnants of Power. The Tragic Last Years of Adlai Stevenson.* New York: Coward-McCann, 1968.

White, Theodore. *The Making of the President, 1960.* New York: New American Library, 1962.

Whitman, Alden. *Portrait, Adlai E. Stevenson: Politician, Diplomat, Friend.* New York: Harper & Row, 1965.

6. Recordings and Films

The student of recent history is fortunate to have available sound recordings and films pertaining to his subject. Contrast this situation with the problem facing the historian of, for example, Thomas Jefferson. He can never know what Jefferson's voice sounded like, or exactly how he looked and acted during any of the crises of his career. But for the student of Stevenson there is a rich collection of records, tapes, and films to supplement the written record. The Stevenson collections at Princeton University and the Illinois State Historical Society each include a large amount of audiovisual material. There also exists a commercially produced conversation between Stevenson and Arnold Michaelis (at Libertyville in June 1956), available through Columbia Records (#D25-793). It is especially important to listen to Stevenson's speeches, because they convey a certain force that cannot be recaptured through reading the texts.